Return on Experience

Return on Experience

By Tim Kobe and Roger Lehman

ORO EDITIONS

Introduction

This book exposes the value of designing human experience. It is written in a question and answer format, to offer insight and context to the answers in the dialogue.

Tim Kobe is founder and CEO of Eight Inc. and founder of X8 Ventures. A design leader, author and business innovator. He frequently speaks about the value creation through design, leading creative teams, and how to bring innovation to business leaders and design team around the world.

A designer by training from the prestigious Art Center College of Design, Tim has earned numerous design awards and frequently lectures globally.

It is co-authored by Roger Lehman, a psychoanalyst and Senior Lecturer at MIT Sloan School of Management as well as a Senior Affiliate professor at INSEAD, France.

This book does not naturally fit into a single category. It will be as comfortable on the shelves of designers and artists as it will on those of business leaders and educators. It reflects the fundamental belief that design is integral to everything we do; that all human existence has been a result of a progression of successful design outcomes. Not in the sense that what we have created is exclusively logical and rational, but in that Eight Inc.'s success has been the result of successful human outcomes. The application of creative emotional intelligence. Meaning being infused into new form that has helped us define human progress and create value.

Inspiration and innovation are difficult to process from a purely logical perspective and require a broader view into the way we think and feel. In some cases, they are deeply personal and at the same time shared at a social level. In this sense, we naturally view design as possessing enormous value and as an essential part of culture, with a broad application.

Design is a dialogue. This book is not a treatise on the do's and don'ts of design or business. It is a reflection on the nature of how to see design. To understand the things we create.

Design is and always has been part of a conversation. As such, this book captures a dialogue I have been engaged in for over 30 years at Eight Inc. This conversation is more than a single path but reflects the dialogue and practice of business leaders, designers, colleagues, and collaborators.

This book would not exist without those on the other side of the conversation and is more than a lens of a single or individual point of view. We have been incredibly fortunate to design with some incredibly sensitive and intelligent people, and to work with some of the world's most successful people and companies. We have been fortunate to create transformational work, and much of our approach I can attribute to a different way of thinking and doing. I think Steve Jobs would agree.

—Tim Kobe

Special thanks to my co-author and Eight Inc. Advisory Board member Roger Lehman.

Thanks to Eight Inc. contributors; Patrick Cox, Matt Judge, Richa Menke, Hilary Clark, Chris Dobson, Simon Smith and Dr. Lorne M. Buchman for their insights and dedication to design. Thank you to the Eight Inc. Advisory Board for guidance and wisdom:

Dr. Chin Nam Tan
Dr. Roger Lehman
Professor Linda Hill
Marwan Abedin
Ovais Naqvi
Christopher E. Kay

Return on Experience Book Design
by Abdul Basit Khan and Yoana Wiman

Apple Genius Bar, Bologna, 2011

Design Human Experience

"Design is not just about how it looks but the way it works"
—Steve Jobs

Apple Store Fifth Avenue, New York, 2006

Apple Store, London, 2006

Apple Macworld, San Francisco, 2007

Apple Store Fifth Avenue, New York, 2006

DEVAS
EXPLOSIVE ON THE WING. HAVOC

Nike Jordan Brand Carmelo Anthony Installation, New York, 2011

Nike Jordan Brand Carmelo Anthony Installation, New York, 2011

Nike Jordan Brand Carmelo Anthony Installation, New York, 2011

Wolff Olins, New York, 2005

Wolff Olins, New York, 2005

Majid Al Futtaim, Wonderbar, Dubai, 2017

Majid Al Futtaim, Wonderbar, Dubai, 2017

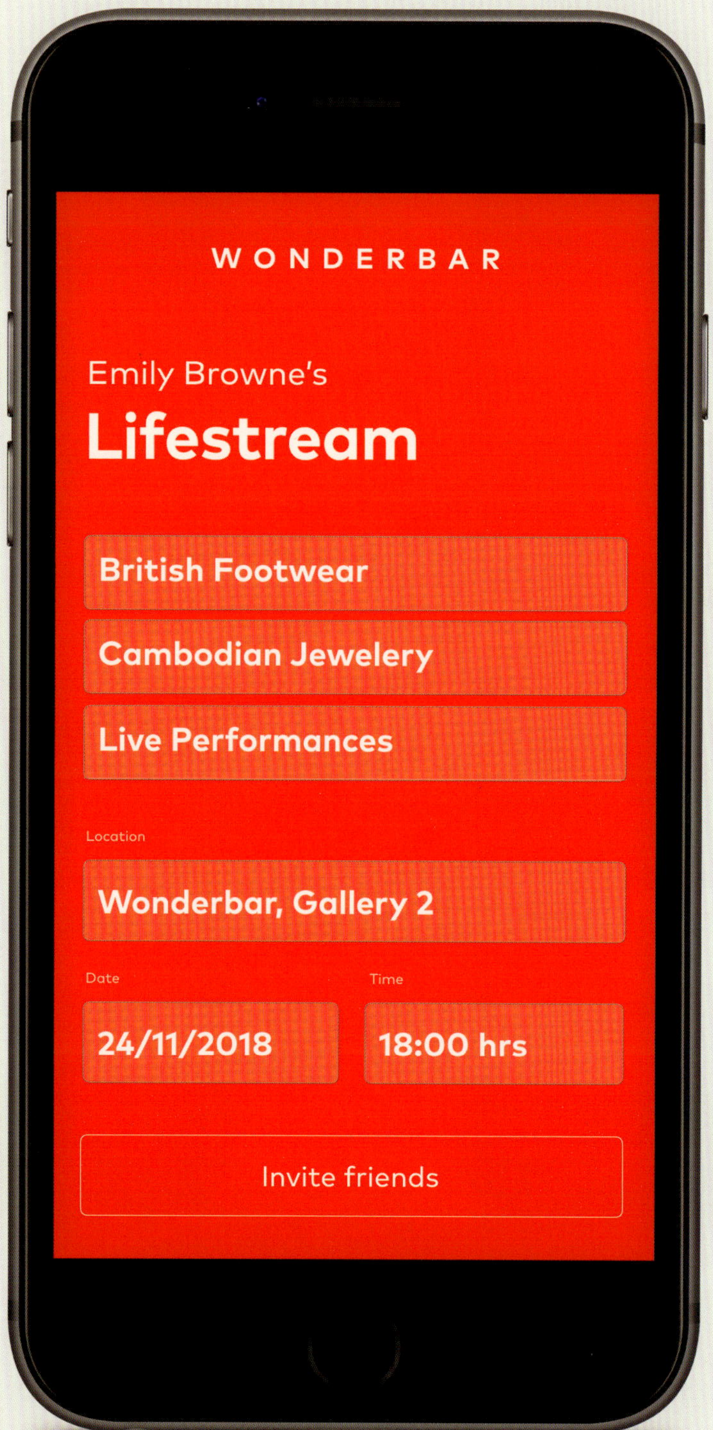
WONDERBAR
Emily Browne's
Lifestream
British Footwear
Cambodian Jewelery
Live Performances
Location
Wonderbar, Gallery 2
Date
24/11/2018
Time
18:00 hrs
Invite friends

Majid Al Futtaim Wonderbar, Dubai, 2017

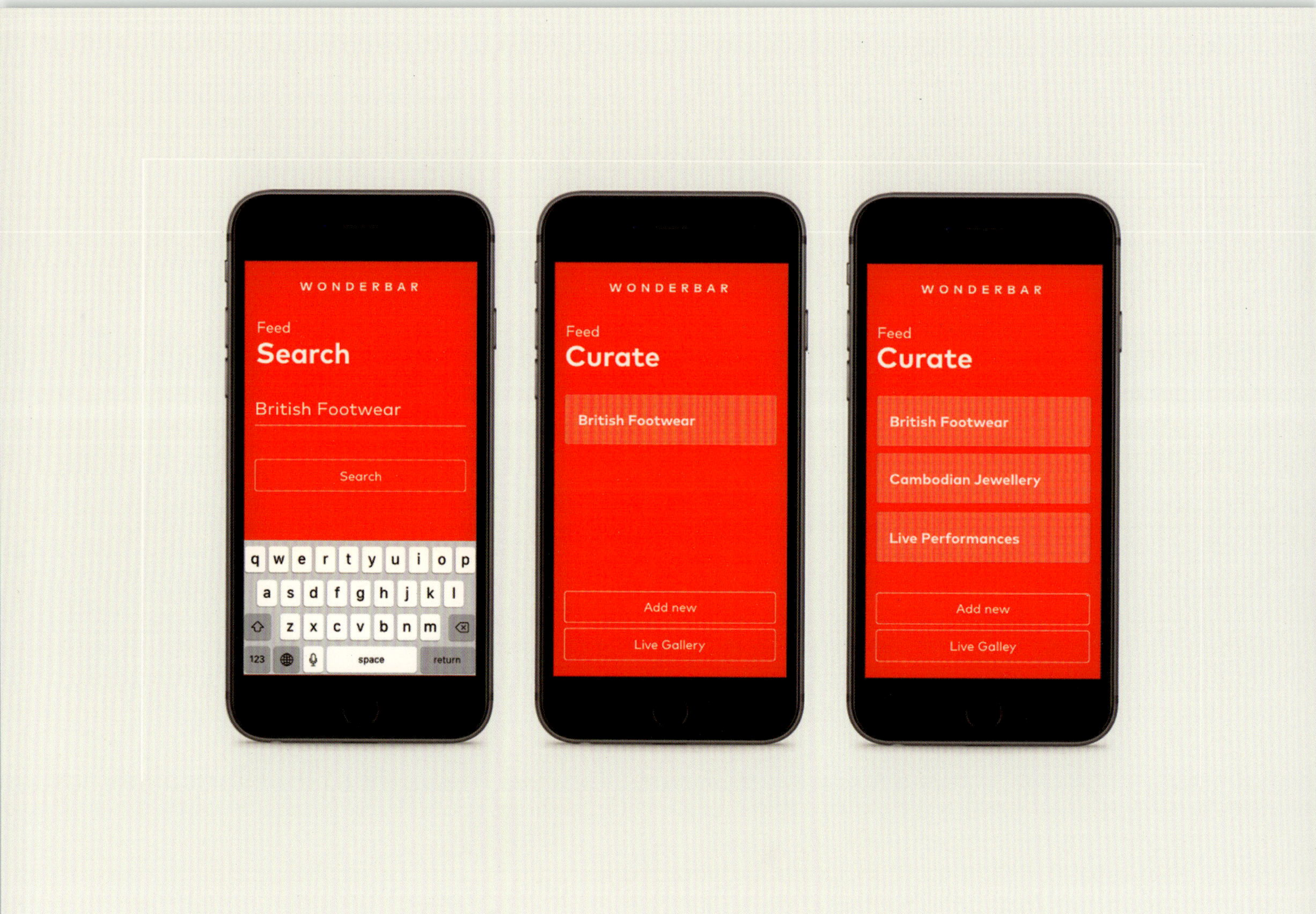

Majid Al Futtaim, Wonderbar, Dubai, 2017

Q: Why is design important?
Other than natural elements, there are very few things we touch in the world today that are not designed. In some cases, even natural things are being reformed—redesigned. Design shapes not just our products but our lives. Behaviors, the environments we live in, services, and our forms and means of communication are created by design. If successful living is important, then the design of that living is essential.

Q: Why Eight Inc.? Where does the idea for Eight Inc. come from?
Eight Inc. is a unique idea. Eight Inc. is a creative collective united by the belief that design defines human progress. It is not about an individual but a group of unique people who share in a belief about design. We created Eight Inc. to be a place that attracts the best creative people. The design and considerations for the studio were to ensure we could deliver high quality, successful design outcomes.

We built it on three primary principles:
1. To create great outcomes from the things we are most interested in.
2. To do meaningful work with the best possible people.
3. To benefit appropriately for the **value we create.**

Value we create. Adding value. A colleague and friend of mine at INSEAD has conducted a great deal of research around the topic of value creation and value destruction (Kaiser & Young, 2013 "The Blue Line Imperative"). Good design creates a positive outcome for people because they intuitively and internally know that it is adding value. It resonates at a deeper level and therefore people "know" that it adds value to their life. This added value perspective connects directly with the "positive outcomes" that result from good design. One could say that "positive outcomes" are the reward for having designed and delivered a product that is perceived as adding value.

Eight Inc. is less an organization and more an organism. It's messy, creative, and dedicated. We are not interested in employing a stylistic approach to design, but more so real design. We don't have creative directors. We have design practitioners, not account managers, who lead our studios. Our work is built on the premise that good design is a design that creates positive outcomes for people.

Q: User-focused design is often discussed but not often successfully practiced. Why?
User-focused design is easily and often cited these days, but difficult to do. Any meaningful design has helped progress the human condition. Progressive thought, curiosity, and humility are fundamental to our success. As a design-led business, Eight Inc. is merely a vehicle for achieving our shared goals: to consistently recognize and respond to the challenges of our clients, (people who are looking to create value and push human progress), our business environment and the world around us.

Q: How is that different from other creative companies?
Eight Inc. is more a practice versus a model or formula. We don't approach our practice in the same way as a branding agency model, research consultancy, or traditional architectural practice. We don't strive to emulate those models. We understand the limitations and benefits of this choice. Externally, this is a different proposition, but is something we believe will separate our group from other approaches. This approach changes the "design" offering and engagement, and moves us to a higher level in the client conversation and value chain. It brings us closer to the leadership of our clients.

I don't believe that today the best design comes from individuals. It's a tired, old idea and has not produced genuinely significant change in recent times. Our approach is designed to produce the best work by bringing the best thought to a project. It requires the diversity of creative inputs from age, race, experience, backgrounds, and gender. Our studio started in California and was influenced by the values and experimentation ethos of the area. A significant influence was the Eames Office, a collective of creative individuals, in Southern California. The Eames Office was not about one person. Of course, there was Charles and Ray Eames leading the office, but it was an incredible group of people who drove the design outcomes of the studio. There is always something stronger in a collaboration of influential design thinkers and doers. If there ever was a framework for what we do, the approach we followed was built around a creative partnership with a diversity of inputs in the spirit of the Eames' Office.

Q: Is all design about the human experience?
I believe you approach design broadly at one level, but it's only truly successful if it can deliver the experience that we imagine is possible. It's critical to create new solutions, but to design these solutions focused on human outcomes. These solutions can transform the basis of understanding and deliver a greater human experience. **Experience** is an outcome of the combination of people, activities, and the context they experience it within.

Experience. Experiences at both an individual and collective level, have to be based on a sense of relationship versus relatedness. Relationship is the result of "feeling felt" often experienced as surprise that the designer thought of something that was so important or resonated so strongly with the individual or with me. When the experience leads to a disconnect it is almost always as a result of a lack of relationship and more of a relatedness which does not take a deep understanding, awareness, connection or appreciation of the other into consideration.

We know that designing a great experience will often lead to extraordinary value. It creates things with human value. Things that matter to people. It will often, as a result, generate economic value, which is usually the by-product of great creative solutions. Good design often connects at both an emotional level and fulfills a **purpose.**

Purpose. The significance of the connection of emotion with purpose is absolutely crucial as this is what generates passion at a level that is often beyond our conscious awareness. It reverberates and resonates at a much deeper level in a way that is often difficult to express in words. We just feel it. Tim frequently refers to this state as one of "irrational loyalty", which is absolutely correct. It is "irrational" because it is an emotional response and not a thinking or rational response to the relationship.

The significance of the connection of emotion with purpose is absolutely crucial as this is what generates passion at a level that is often beyond our conscious awareness. It reverberates and resonates at a much deeper level, in a way that is often difficult to express in words. We just feel it. This may seem soft and difficult to quantify, and it is essentially what designers are best equipped to determine. Design defines objects, places, and ultimately human experience.

Q: Design can mean many things. What is design to you?
Design is change. At a high level, the best design reflects the challenges of the time we live in and improves upon them. It's a reflection of who we are, our values, and our inventiveness. It relates to how we use our

resources most effectively. It is defined by a history of progress and anticipates and defines a future. Design is an incredibly valuable part of human progress. It helps drive the human race forward. Design is not just for those who are educated in design but is in concert with engineers and builders or craftsmen in order to create effective new solutions. It can be through small changes or dramatic innovation. All growth comes from creative thought applied to our shared challenges. Creativity is not something for a select few, but rather something that we all can participate in. Yet to design requires a skill. Historically, design has been significantly under-appreciated in business but has likely added the most value to human experience and success. Creativity is one of the core human attributes that have led to our survival as a **species.**

Species. There are two fundamental types of thinking, causal and associative. Causal thinking is the more common in organizations. It is "cause and effect" and focuses on understanding the "why" by conducting a "root cause" analysis. Associative thinking is much less structured and is less common in most organizations. However, associative thinking is more prominent in the creation of good design as well as in problem solving and creativity. Instead of asking "why?" as in causal thinking, associative thinking asks "what comes to mind?" It does not immediately seek to find the answer but rather to explore the options, the alternatives, the different possibilities and scenarios. An organization is more causal focused while an organism operates more from an associative perspective. For the most part, creativity emerges out of the associative rather than the causal approach.

Design as a skill is as fundamental as is any other acquired practice. One problem with defining what design is has to do with its range. It can exist at a vast scale or ambition for any particular thing.

Design. The skill of design is the capacity to balance causal and associative thinking perspectives and to move between these two modes of problem solving in a fluid manner based on the task at hand. Both causal and associative thinking are necessary in order to deliver great design.

To understand design, we need to look at the many dimensions of design. It is commonly seen as creating form or shape, a decorative layer, a look or feel, a building form, or an object. It is widely under-valued and not understood well. Design is often confused with engineering, and that is primarily because we tend to want to label and codify things to understand them. It is also a strategy for value extraction often used in business. Design is much more vibrant than this. In essence, it is the way we solve for conditions that need to be better.

Because it is a process and a creative intervention to address human challenges, design can be more **rich** by finding new solutions: taking ideas to actions that people need, want, and want to adopt.

Rich. Design can be much richer because it is based on associative thinking and therefore resonates at a different level, one which builds a sense of feeling felt and therefore builds a personal connection and a sense of relationship with others or with the product.

To create value and progress requires the ability to see a wide range of complex factors that influence the experience people will have and simplify it to its essential elements. What you define as the essential elements may be rational or **emotional.**

Emotional. The rational and emotional might be seen as manifestations of causal and associative thinking. Most often the resonance of good design is based on a combination of the causal with the associative parts of our experience—both the functional and emotional parts of our existence are activated at a deeper level which resonates with our sense of value creation.

Design has a conscience—both for critical analysis but also memory. It has been one of the most critical aspects of creating the way we live today. It's a responsibility for the future that we all share. The ability to define and create things that improve our lives requires core skills a nd the ability to work across traditional disciplines—it is something everyone can be a part of. The most successful companies of today are not the same ones from years past and will likely not be the most valuable ones in the future.

Q: Is design a tool to change culture in the way other art forms do?
I think we are seeing a more significant shift in the understanding of what design can do for people. Design can create value that transforms the way we live and addresses unresolved human and environmental issues. Design thrives at the intersection of art and science. Steve Jobs and Apple always held that belief. Design is different from art in the sense it serves a purpose or function. Both share intent. Art and design both offer transformative tools to change the way we think and do things. I believe design may be one of the greatest ways to drive transformation in culture because of its immediacy and accessibility. It is a fundamental task that drives humanity.

Q: Design seems to be taking a larger role in culture and business. What types of things are driving this shift?
Effective design is always about **change.**

Change. The crucial aspect of change is not the change itself which is an event, but the transition, which is how we as humans navigate that change. Change can happen almost instantaneously, however the transition, how people interpret, integrate and adapt to the change can take weeks, months or years… or in extreme cases, never be accepted. (Bridges, 2004)

We have been operating in a very old model, both in the way we understand the value of design and those who we hold up as examples of what a successful designer is. I do not believe in the idea that star architects or star designers can produce truly meaningful or relevant work. Small thoughts of self are never big ideas. If it were a viable design model, we would live in a much better world.

Granted there are wonderful examples of great architecture and design, but it is only through the experience of these examples that we understand them. Much of the shift is around the recognition of what quality architecture or design can offer. Both ideally come from a human outcome perspective and then what the value creation outcomes are. The Design's ascent to occupy a more significant role in business comes from the success of companies who are driven from a customer or user perspective gaining a competitive advantage by being more **relevant.**

Relevant. The significance here is the importance of "being more relevant." Companies that are driven from a customer or user perspective understand that they need to build a meaningful relationship with their consumers. This implies that the connection resonates for both parties at a positive emotional experience level, and that there is a sense of "being understood" or of "feeling felt." Companies who do not understand the importance of this dynamic will approach their consumers in a detached, instrumental, non-emotional manner, resulting in the customer or user feeling disconnected, misunderstood and not valued or appreciated.

Q: Many people think design is about the form or materials of something. Is this fundamentally what design is?
Design is often understood—most commonly in the consumption society—as a superficial thing. The form, color, or finish of something. Most things that exist primarily at a surface level may not be essential or meaningful. As such, this has fundamentally limited the perception of the value of design. The form and materials are the most common

reference to design but are a basic level of understanding. Great design, regardless of the category, is often rooted in more profound meaning and ultimately cultural or personal value. Architecture is the same. Often designers and architects work to define a style and clients look for a specific "style" that they feel defines their individuality. While this is often easier for clients as a consumable, for those who may not understand the value of the work it reduces the perception and appreciation of the design to something that is misleading concerning real value creation.

Q: So design is more than what we see?
Things we see and touch are the most fundamental aspects of design and therefore the most **familiar.**

Familiar. In fact, we know at a gut level quite literally, (see *The Mind-Gut Connection* by Emeran Mayer, 2016) when something is 'right', when it is perceived as being value adding. TThis process is not initiated by our rational, intellectual self but indeed comes more out of awareness, a "gut feeling". When we tune in and actually listen to it, we clearly know which designs resonate deeply within us and therefore add value for us, and which do not.

It is much more than a form or a material decision. This is something that seems intangible, but there are ways to recognize when it's right. All design is change, but not all change is necessary or valuable. Design possesses value when change occurs and through change there is adoption. People need to find it important. At a basic level design serves a pure function. The stone wheel served a pure purpose but the wheel has since been designed to address far broader functions and use cases. Design can be specific to a particular set of needs and desires. Antonio Gaudi was not widely appreciated during his lifetime for the architectural contributions he made for Barcelona. It is hard to imagine Barcelona today without Gaudi's work though, or film without Alfred Hitchcock.

Significant work of any type contributes to carrying forward a thought or conversation. Great work is often obvious in retrospect.

Q: What is the connection between design and experience?
Design is fundamentally a creative endeavor for a purpose. That is, not just people but the context of our immediate and broader environment. Without a guiding philosophy that is rooted in the change of things

for the better, we can't achieve the full potential of design. As a broad term, many people fail to understand what the possibility of design is and think of it in historical terms. Design is more than just a function. It can be useful to drive people's behavior and to achieve a higher state of **being.** Newmeyer's States of Being describes participation and engagement as the most base levels of satisfaction, but productivity, happiness, and wellbeing are the top of the pyramid.

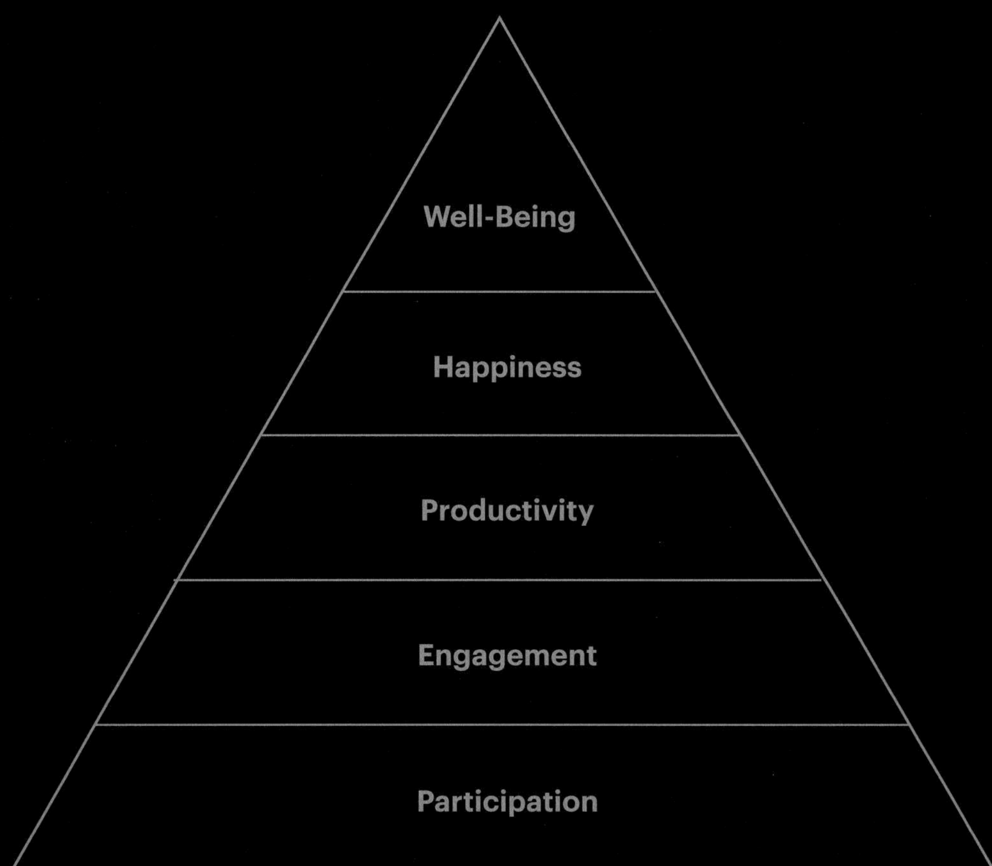

Newmeyer's *States of Being* Diagram

Being. Indeed Newmeyer's States of Being and identifying participation and engagement at the most basic level of satisfaction connects closely with the concept of Fair Process. We know that people will be more engaged and motivated if they are able to contribute to the process by which decisions are made. We also know that decisions made by a group or teams are almost always superior to those made by an individual (See *The Wisdom of Crowds*, by James Surowiecki, 2005).

The Fair Process model is a circular decision-making tool providing a structure for this approach by identifying five necessary steps. All five of these steps are achieved through the engagement and participation of those for whom the decision is significant and whose input will enrich the exploration and decision process. Fair Process starts from the position that the leader or designer does not necessarily have the best idea or solution, even though they ultimately may make the final decision.

The first step in Fair Process is for the leader or designer to engage the relevant stakeholders in identifying what is the task, question or issue to be addressed. This engaging and framing of the issue or task creates the space for an open exploration which might well generate new and more creative ideas or options in terms of what the issue really is. This is also the space for more associative thinking in which no idea is considered "wrong" or "bad" and often the ideas of one person spark a creative perspective in another. It is a form of focused brainstorming to frame the issue.

Step 2 is the exploration and elimination of the options that have been surfaced in Step 1. Not all ideas are equal and even very creative and useful ideas might just not be realistic or appropriate given the context, resources, or time pressures. The point is that all steps should take place in an open and transparent environment. In other words the leader or designer should engage all in the process of exploring and eliminating options, which is the primary focus of Step 2.

However, where this often breaks down is with the setting of expectations, which is Step 3. Inevitably there will be someone who is disappointed that their idea was not adopted or who thinks that the chosen idea or solution is inferior. The setting of expectations means that it is explicitly stated that even if one is not in agreement with the choice, they now need to agree to whole-heartedly participate in its implementation. If they are unable to make that commitment, they need to be removed from the implementation team. (For example a CEO sent two members of his executive board to deliver a road show of the new strategy, even though they thought it was inferior to their strategic ideas, with the clear expectation that they would successfully present his new strategy and if they were not successful,there was no need for them to return to HQ... which they did)

Step 4 is implementation. It is another point where many organizations fail. The classic Step 4 comment is "I know we've decided but I think I can tweak it just a bit more and make it even better". As a result, the decision or product never moves further down the path to implementation but is constantly being "improved". The role of the leader/designer is to point out that there will be plenty of opportunity for improvement in Step 5, when the team moves into Evaluation and Learning and then the process starts all over again with Step 1.

At its best, design creates positive outcomes. At its best, you feel it's right. It resonates at levels of beauty, essentialness and value. Communities depend on a diversity of talent in the same way design relies on a variety of sensitivities to engage with our rational and emotional responses. The potential of **great design** is to change the way we think about the things around us. It can change the way we feel and do things.

Great design. What we identify as "Great Design" is usually "great" because it resonates at a deeper level of meaning and purpose, often outside of our conscious (immediate) awareness. "Great Design" like "great art" resonates internally but is not easily explained. In some manner, it speaks to our basic common interest. Our need to both belong and be differentiated, to be challenged and inspired, to have the experience of the design resonating within us in a manner which is not easily expressed in words but more likely felt at an emotional level.

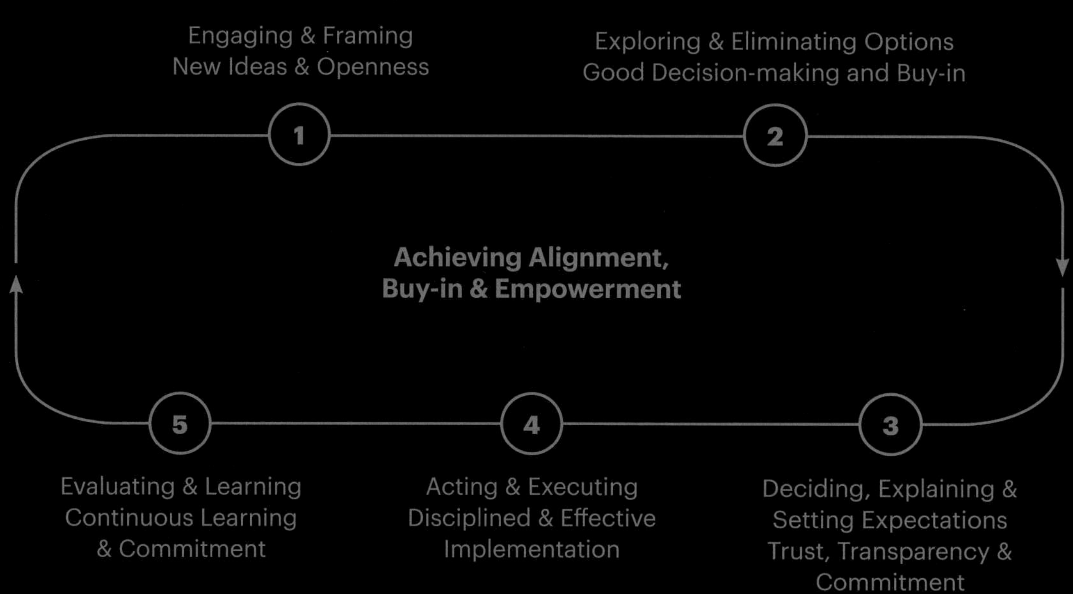

Fair Process Diagram
Source: Ludo Van der Heyden, INSEAD

Q: Design is typically defined by a category: architecture, industrial design, interior design, etc. Can you talk about your rejection of these traditional disciplines?
We don't reject them. We see the limitations, but we don't reject disciplines. Discipline structure makes it easier to organize and provide focus and depth in education. It's fine for education but limiting in practice. We have moved beyond that way of thinking. We used to talk about a multi- or trans-disciplinary approach. We practiced a form of design that was what we see as a more relevant way of creating things. Since this process and method has helped us create a more effective design we have moved to the idea of being anti-disciplinary. The importance of an anti-**disciplinary** approach is that it invites and encourages ideas from all participants interacting. This can only be done in an "anti-disciplinary" environment.

Disciplinary. This concept resonates very much with the perspective of Ronald Heifetz in terms of *Adaptive Leadership* (2009). Heifetz's perspective is that the task of the leader or designer is not to have the best ideas but rather to create an environment which is open to all new and different perspectives in order to find the best solution.

Our focus is not on the education structure of our past. It's essential to create new things if we apply the same structure to the problem. It is often how people naturally experience things. We holistically experience everything. To create a new successful experience you must look outside of convention or category norms.

Most designers are trained in a specific discipline, but human experience is not limited to an educational channel. Most of us have been trained in a method that is reminiscent of the industrial era. Our lives today are very different to the categorical structure that sees people as a single cog in the wheel. I think we may see people differently. We look at those categories as a product of the industrial era.

Maybe the simplest way of thinking about design is to focus on making things that matter. As I mentioned earlier, it is a function of our education system but not necessarily the way we live. It is a sort of remedial way of thinking and classifying by using categories. It's fairly primitive. People often look at design by thinking they need a building or an interior, so they hire that specialist. It relates to the "professionalization" of creative services, which certainly has regrettable outcomes, yet may be the most common way of thinking about structure and order.

Q: What is the human aspect of design?
All design is about creating an outcome. It must have purpose. **Human outcomes** change the way we live.

Human outcomes. The question that every organization and designer should be asking themselves is "what is our primary task?". The primary task of the Apple store is to create a very unique customer experience in which the customer feels more like a co-creator and a member of the "community" than a customer. Selling computers, watches and phones is a result of having created this very unique culture within the Apple store. Sales is a result of getting the primary task correct. Unfortunately, most organizations identify their primary task as being one of either making a profit or of selling so many units of a product. This immediately creates a disconnect with the customer because the focus is not on the customer experience. However, associated with every "primary task" there is the "primary risk", the risk of failure, of getting it wrong. Clever leaders and designers know that their role is to be able to identify and acknowledge the risk and yet push the boundaries of development and innovation. As Jeff Bezos says, "If you know it's going to work, it's not an experiment". This creates the space for experimentation and learning.

I was asked about the value of humanities in our era of STEM-focused education and whether we need to study humanities. Why are we studying STEM? Who is it for? Why is it important? If not the humanities, then what are we working for? If we are not designing for people, their activities, and the environment we live in, then what is the point of a great scientific progress or a new algorithm? All of our endeavors must add value to the human experience or we are simply missing the real opportunity. This is where design becomes incremental and less focused on value creation.

To design for a more human relevance is to recognize people and their behavior. Businesses often tend to classify people. We tend to look at **human behavior.**

Human behavior. Once again we see the relevance of *The Blue Line Imperative: What Managing for Value Really Means*; (Kaiser and Young, 2013) and of the importance of adding value, not from our perspective but rather from the perspective of the consumer, client or customer. The critical aspect here is the capacity to "meet the other where they are" and to then be able to take them to where they never imagined was possible.

Marshall McLuhan says categories do not drive behavior but it is better not to design for narrow roles like "users" or "consumers." People are far more interesting and more complex than that. The more we **understand ourselves** the better we can create useful solutions.

Understand ourselves. Self-awareness is a critical asset in this entire process. Leaders and designers need to be able to tap into what is happening below the surface, both in themselves and in the others with whom they are engaged. The greater the self-awareness, the more effective one is in "meeting the other where they are".

Patrick Cox, Eight Inc. Chief Innovation Officer talks about not needing to design in artificially imposed disciplines, or think purely about "digital" or "physical" interactions within silos. Reality is more fluid and interconnected than that. All design is about a transformation from something to something new. Without a purpose it is not design. It can be art, but it's not design.

Q: How does the human focus contribute to creating value?
A well-designed experience helps connect people with places and things. If this is created strategically, it can maintain that relationship and be successful. Financial success is commonly a product of a compelling offer and experience that produces a human outcome. However, financial targets are not our primary goal. They are the result of successful human outcomes. The design goals should be more about making things that matter to people. In many cases, this means transforming the ways businesses work. Look at *The Blue Line Imperative*. If you are focused on the human value, making all of the decisions around the experience to serve the needs of people involved, you will build value.

The Apple retail program, for example, as a critical touch point for the company, is designed as a clear expression of the values of the company. The connection between Apple, its customers, and the people that admire and connect with the values of the brand is something that happens through a combination of things we understand naturally.

Human beings are holistic creatures. People can experience these things in many ways, but a holistic approach delivers something **distinct** for Apple or any other companies who express their values to others.

Distinct. There's an aspect of "co-creation" taking place at the Apple store. It's not just the staff or the products but the level of engagement and interaction of the staff with and between the 'participants' (visitors to the Apple store don't see themselves as "customers" but as co-creators who actively and consciously engage in the process of co-creating the community.) Entering an Apple store is entering into a community, whether the store is in the US, Singapore, France, Germany, or anywhere else in the world.

Q: Designing experience is about interactions?
There is a natural response that people have thorough interactions. Human interactions create innate physical and emotional responses. Threat, compared to acts of generosity, produce different chemical reactions in our bodies and lead to entirely different results. Our emotional feedback contributes in a massive way to our behavior. When you look at the objectives of experience, you have to examine the psychological and physiological effect of the interaction.

Q: Eight Inc. works with some of the best-known and best-loved companies in the world. What makes some companies loved more by their customers than others?
Trust. Respect. Things that make any relationship work. Great companies can develop relationships with their customers and deliver products or services that are experienced on both rational and emotional levels. Great companies are loved because they can be trusted to do that on a reliable basis. When the products and services no longer deliver, loyalty disappears and trust declines. The challenge is to remain focused on what customers experience with the products and services if you want people to be passionate about the relationship.

Q: What makes for an exceptional connected relationship?
Experience is at the core of any significant relationship. How you interact. What you share and why you connect. The same thing that makes successful relationships. Mutual trust and respect are fundamental. The success of a project depends on how well the team members, clients, designers, and consultants understand and engage with each other. Companies who are most adaptable at working with creative teams also understand the dynamics of their organizations, their strengths and limitations. **Moving** from the status quo to a new business model or a new design execution is often one of the most common struggles teams have.

Moving. It is at this stage (moving from the status quo to a new business model) where ideas and innovation often falters. Fear of failure overwhelms the key decision makers and all of a sudden there are 1,000 reasons for not pursuing the innovation or new design. We refer to these processes as "social defenses".

Much like the individual defense mechanisms that we all employ when we are feeling uncertain or under threat of attack, teams and organizations also employ unconscious collective defense mechanisms in order to avoid their fear of failure. Common examples of such social defenses are: calling in yet another consultant or an additional expert, rigidly applying process, endless meeting where no decision is made, overwhelming amount of spreadsheets and data, covert coalitions, committing to a strategy but not actually following through with the behavior to support it, and many other behaviors that teams and organizations employ in order to avoid the anxiety they are facing.

It is primarily due to companies not being set up to disrupt themselves easily. Accountability and compensation structures typically limit the most dramatic changes and keep companies from really disrupting their business model. This can dramatically affect design decisions that are not based on the user. This is the difference between the best-loved companies and the **others.**

Others. The best loved, most successful companies that continue to grow and evolve have figured out how to manage the risk of failure. By addressing it openly, all involved can get on with their "primary task" rather than being derailed by the anxiety that is always present and accentuated when risk goes unacknowledged.

Apple Watch Launch, Cupertino, 2014

Change

**Proposing possible design solutions is not hard.
Designing successful solutions is remarkably hard.**

Apple Watch Launch, Cupertino, 2014

Apple Watch Launch, Cupertino, 2014

EXIT

Apple Watch Launch, Cupertino, 2014

tv
Now with HD movie rentals. Coming to a living room near you.
Macworld
1300
Macworld
1400

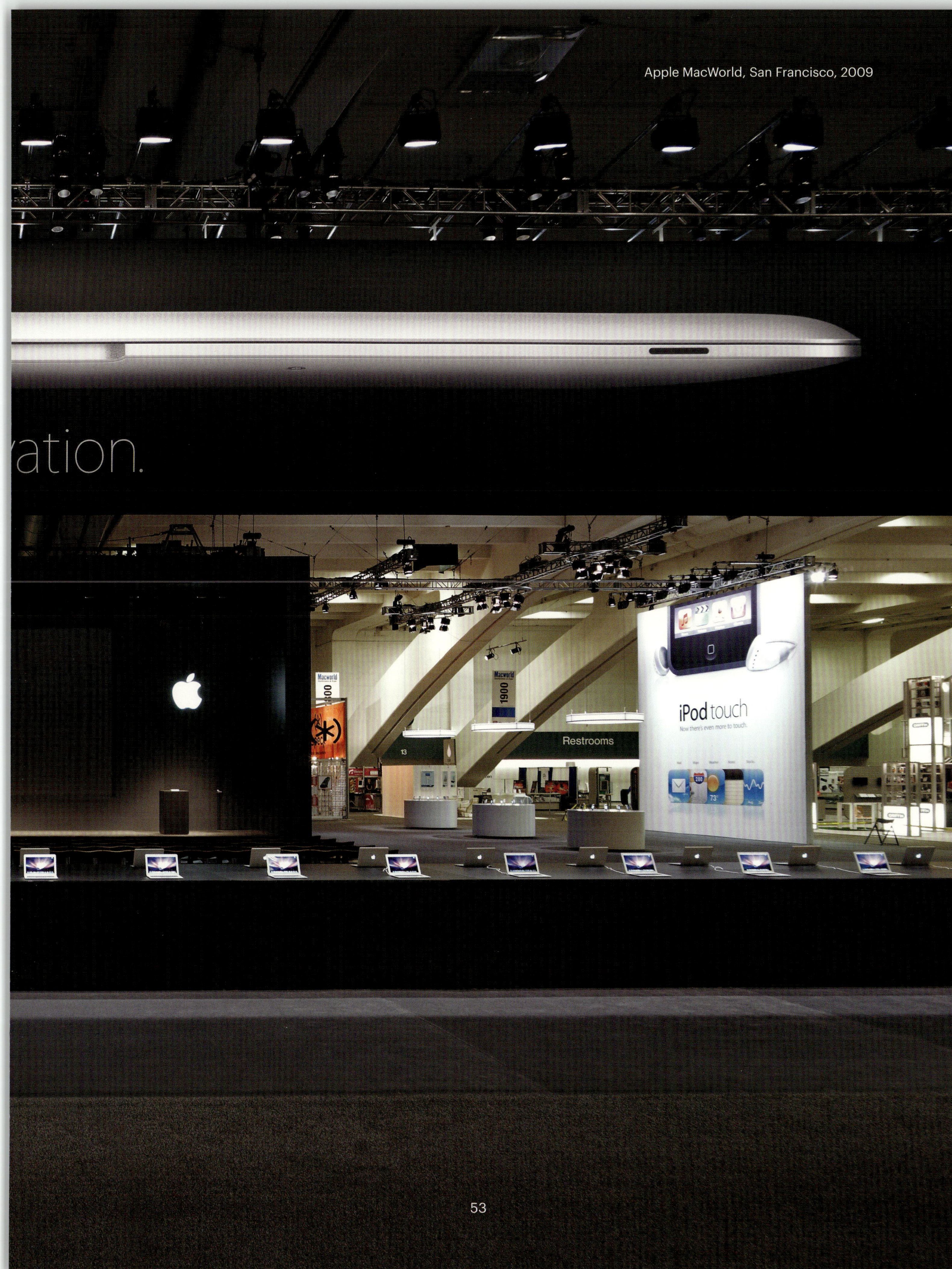

Apple MacWorld, San Francisco, 2009

Apple MacWorld, San Francisco, 1999

Apple MacWorld, San Francisco, 1999

PowerBook G3
Think different.

Apple MacWorld, San Francisco, 1999

Apple MacWorld, New York, 2000

Apple MacWorld, New York, 2000

Apple Store, Palo Alto, 2001

Q: What are the most prominent challenges designers face when trying to create new ways for companies to engage with their customers?
Change. It's **fundamentally** the most challenging thing people have to deal with in life and certainly in business. It's also the most difficult aspect of design to manage.

Fundamentally. Bridges's concept of change mentioned in Chapter 1 focuses on the importance of the transition that always accompanies change. The idea is that the major task in any change is not the change itself but how individuals navigate the transition that is necessary for them to embrace the change. It is the transition that is the most problematic for people when confronted with a change. The crucial role in all organizations as well as design projects is the necessity to have someone who can help the people being impacted by the change to understand and navigate the transition.

It becomes more difficult the more extensive the scope of the solution is. In some cases a design solution is about change at many levels in an organization: at the brand values level, the behavioral level, with the business structure, or the interaction level, and sometimes it's all of these things. Except for those trained in understanding the humanities—musicians, artists, writers, designers etc.—few people are well equipped to deal with change.

There is very little in today's education to prepare people to deal with change or progress. Training for understanding people seems to be of lower and lower priority in the education system in the US for example, and it is primarily the reason the most successful companies exist. Ironically it is the ability to deal with change that may add the most value and determine a successful outcome.

Q: Why is change important in design?
All design is about change in either large or small ways. It's one reason good designers are so **valuable** in a time where business is being disrupted.

Valuable. The fundamental issue here is whether or not people perceive the change as being "value adding" or "value destroying", which is very much an individual as well as a collective process. (See Quy Huy on "Collective Emotions" (1999)). If the general perception is that the change is not value adding, then you can bet on resistance to the change at the overt as well as covert levels.

The problem is that people are creatures of habit who find comfort in ritual and repetitive behavior. Most desire a linear, predictable, easier path. There is not much desire for ambiguity or risk, but all new things possess ambiguity and perception of risk at the beginning. Validation in business, or personally, is a product of understanding how we fit into the world. People look for stability and security in their place. The problem is the business landscape keeps changing. The world keeps changing.

Q: Is this what makes design difficult for companies to embrace?
Change is a fundamental part of progress. It is difficult for people, companies and governments. We see it in the form of backlash in many of the political arenas seen around the world, historically and today. If access to information is no longer a problem, then filtering and sorting the meaningful from the noise becomes a capability everyone should possess. Flexibility is also an inherently difficult condition to deal with because it's easier to frame a clear linear structure and implement it. We understand things within the physical metrics of mathematics language, but there is also something else at play we know less about. **Intuition** is engaging a part of our brain that does not have the capability for language.

Intuition. Understanding the Blue Line and the Red Line (Kaiser & Young) is essential here. We all know at the most basic level what is value adding and what is value destroying. We often refer to this as gut feelings or intuition, but sadly we tend to ignore or rationalize our way out of acknowledging what we "know to be true".

It is not the new neocortex part of the brain but the limbic or more primal portion that drives behavior. It's responsible for trust and understanding, qualities that are difficult to process in any other way.

Q: Does design serve as a challenger to the status quo?
Design is ultimately a catalyst and a methodology for change. It requires asking difficult questions and challenging conventional assumptions. It is not bad but can be uncomfortable depending on the assignment. It is often inspired by, and is the creator of, things that are anti-normal by definition. Change is incredibly difficult for most people but designers have a unique skill set that finds optimism and power in change. Design is about change but the right strategies are dependent on the kind of problem or organization.

It's essential to apply the right tool to the right job. This means understanding the commitment you are asking people to make, and the level of that commitment. The complexity can be a challenge and to understand the most important narratives in a project becomes critical. This may be both high-level macro narratives and the individual personal ones. The majority of design will have an impact on existing systems and organizations, and the roles people play in organizations may be impacted by what you do. It can be hard to justify the proposals unless you look at the greater good. You have a choice to participate in that change depending on the outcome objective. We usually see this as part of a greater master plan. We typically frame this into an Experience Master Plan.

Companies don't hire strategic designers to change the color of the wall or the material on the floor to help make it more appetizing for a target audience. It's generally understood that superficial change is no change at all. Banks, airlines or other more conservative large scale organizations are among the most challenging organizations to change. To create any great customer experience, we must also be relevant in the mindset of the customers and their changing values. In addition to extreme shifts in the behavior and expectations of millennials, the banking industry has never been more at risk and disrupted by players within and outside the category. The ambition has been defined as a transformative one, one that reflects a dynamic new culture that supports deeper and more meaningful **relationships.**

Relationships. And that "more meaningful relationship" is experienced as being value adding, special, significant, and we feel personally connected.

Q: Do competitors see this as an opportunity to challenge the established businesses?

A new experience can have an enormous impact on organizations because it touches all of the points where customers are. With banks, as transactions have moved to mobile devices distributed everywhere, the physical space needs to become one of the vital places to connect people and to distinguish the services that banks can offer. Meaningful engagement begins with a clear purpose. Its purpose is to serve the customers needs with the best possible method. It has to recognize diverse tasks to question each traditional banking function and define new ones that can separate them from their competition.

At Apple, the core value of the business was always best represented when the product and the software worked in harmony to deliver the best experience. Not just about form or finish or thickness of the object, because without the meaning the experience provides, the form and finish become a hollow discussion. The same is true in architecture and other types of touch points businesses have with their customers. Few remember the tech specs of the first iPod. Most remember 1,000 songs in your pocket.

Q: You worked with Steve Jobs from the year he returned to Apple in 1997 until he stepped away from the business. How was he to work with?
Steve Jobs has been described many ways. Many tried to limit him in some ways by their descriptions of their experience with him. I'm confident Steve was pretty limitless. He understood how to create value and how to approach real problems. To have empathy for people using technology has always been a core Apple characteristic: make it easy to use and simple to understand. It had to be human-centric first, not tech-centric. He took machines out the hands of the engineers and gave them to everyone. Not everyone understood what Steve was doing. Some of those who did understand hated him for it. To be able to have clear focus and clarity around a product's fundamental human value was something he could inherently understand and deliver. It has always allowed for the best possible execution of an idea, but Apple traditionally focused on it as a primary objective. Communication of the human value not the tech spec was another pillar. The ability to convey the message of the "why" in all forms and touch points and to "**impute**" the values of the company has allowed Apple to move from a functional brand ideal to an aspirational one.

Impute Impute from Mark Markula's marketing structure from the early Apple formation days.

We truly loved working with him, even in the most challenging times. And there were challenging times. He challenged everyone and everything. Our greatest regret is he is no longer working to solve the incredible array of issues we face today. We miss him very much.

Q: Are these qualities distinct to Apple's success?
Most companies are either creating, leveraging or destroying value. Apple's success has always been derived from creating compelling human outcomes. Any company must stay true to that or it will not be as valuable as it can be. All design success comes from results based on these outcomes. Steve knew this, and many other people who are admired in business or design reflect this; Richard Branson, Elon Musk, and many other respected business leaders deliver on human outcomes. It is a common thread with many of the people we are engaged with across many business categories, cultures or geographies.

Q: Did this experience impact your business?
Every client relationship provides an opportunity to learn. We have to maintain a continuous learning attitude. I have to say the work for Apple has been a vital demonstration of an approach to creating value. It was a source of pride with the team involved and has been a focus and case study within our group. We learned a great deal from every engagement and each would not have been as successful without the challenging and thoughtful people we worked with. The experience we gained early in our business, working with extraordinary people like Robert Mondavi (Napa Valley winemaking pioneer) and Julia Child (American chef and food pioneer) allowed us to understand how to work on the next design. We learned how to work with people who challenge you as a matter of practice. To see if you were clear enough within your thought to defend what you believed in when you were challenged, and to have a Plan B. Many of the great people we work with demand a clear strategy before we design and are successful because of this sort of hard practice.

Q: Apple has been a significant client for you for many years. Can you talk about the range of things you have been involved with for Apple?
When Steve returned as CEO we were one of three strategic, creative firms working for Apple (the others: CKS providing the branding and communications work with Tom Suiter and Andy Dreyfus, and TBWA with Lee Clow who led Apple's advertising work). For the majority of that time, we were responsible for anything three-dimensional that was not

a product or communications including product launches, events, point of sale, all channel touch points, and the design for the global retail program. Local architects and other designers were brought in for peer review, feedback and local implementation of the retail stores. 2019 was our 22nd year engaged with Apple.

Q: Eight Inc. began working with Apple by designing the Apple MacWorld events?
Yes. We were initially hired in 1997 when Steve returned to Apple to design the MacWorld trade show for the launch of the first colored iMacs. We were introduced to Steve by the team at CKS who led the branding work at that time and were asked to look at the MacWorld global design program and product launch that was being planned. We were asked to define the new physical space to launch the Apple products. As well as to the retail program, we continue to design the MacWorld events and product launches globally. Originally the MacWorld events were the essential touchpoints for Apple to convey their brand and new product offers to customers. Our concept was to create a simple, large scale space with basic geometric form to present the products. By keeping the geometry simple we were able to allow light and the forms of the display to be a backdrop to feature the experience of the product. To allow the product, which at that time was the colored iMacs, to be the hero.

We designed the space to allow for a dramatic perspective of the product and presented the translucent iMacs on continuous light tables that ran the length of the space—to experience Apple products beyond a technology appliance and to elevate its magic and beauty. Our solution was to place the translucent plastic products on an architectural fixture, essentially a light table and to let the products glow. The design gave the product an element of drama and elevated it to an object of desire. By recognizing the inherent value of the product and presenting it to be experienced in a remarkable way was key. I believe this was one of the first times the category was perceived as a consumer product versus a utilitarian piece of equipment.

Q: Some may remember the MacWorld events at the annual convergence of the Apple culture. How did the design language

you created for the events translate into the brand qualities?
Fundamentally the brand qualities were translated into the design of the experience. These events were the primary way Apple could communicate with its community of loyal followers and attract new customers. There has always been an incredible amount of passion and anticipation created at each event, for new products, but also because they defined a new way forward for technology. The events had different purposes than retail, but the idea's simplicity and clarity translated into the spaces and the event experience became core to what the brand was about.

If you are creating successful design, then the loyalty that can be generated is a very valuable outcome. Many companies look to create preference. Preference is good, but passion is so much better. If a design can communicate qualities about the company that build passion and loyalty, then it has done its job. We know effective experience has enormous tangible benefits. Temkin research found that people are "six times more likely to buy with a positive emotional experience, 12 times more likely to recommend the company, and 5 times more likely to forgive a mistake." This beats preference every time. The value of loyalty that exceeds rational thought is powerful because of the way we behave. We tend to act emotionally and justify behavior rationally. It is an interesting human quality but is real and tangible when applied to designing human experience.

Q: Eight Inc. is well known for designing the Apple retail stores. Can you describe how that came about?
The retail program began from two insights. We truly believed in the values Apple represented as a company long before we were ever hired. We never allowed other types of computers in our studios. We shared the belief that technology must be accessible and integral in ways that traditional hardware and software products were not. The second was a realization that only by controlling the relationship could Apple compete with the others given the limitations of traditional ways technology was being sold. This meant we could extend the Apple culture in a way that was more distinctive and gave the opportunity to create more profound experiences for people to develop relationships with Apple.

We began the program initially from a strategy point of view. My white paper on Apple flagship retail presented the view on the opportunity I believed the company possessed. We had seen how Apple had been poorly represented and sold in traditional channel retail, and recognized the Apple retail program must become a more significant touch-point with the Apple community. The insight for Apple came from the exposure to the shift in the retail business model that manufacturers were dealing with in other categories. Our previous clients, The North Face and Nike, were experiencing similar challenges with others representing their message and values.

Q: Why did you think Apple should have its own flagship retail program?
I believed there was an excellent opportunity for Apple to redefine the conversation with their customers and control the relationship in a more meaningful way. When we discussed this with Steve it was understood as a way to move from the traditional way of defining computers as utilitarian devices, to defining Apple as a more aspirational brand by creating a new definition of their core values. Essentially creating the space and experience for conveying the Apple story.

It came to Apple owning the relationship with their customers, the people who shared Apple's values and those who potentially did. In each of our previous retail clients, and similarly with Apple, third-party retail channels were not delivering in the best interests of the brand but commonly what was in the best interest of the reseller business. Other categories of retail were moving into their own stores as a way to control the conversation with their customers. In each case potential buyers of Nike or The North Face were driven to a touchpoint but only to be counter-sold by the channel representative. We identified the core problems Apple's retail presence was facing. It was inconsistent and lacked the "retail tools" to adequately convey the Apple message.

It was competing in a Wintel-defined retail environment at that time and Apple had a relatively low market share (about 2%). As such, it had limited influence on method of presentation or role in the conversation. Resellers were often counter-selling other higher margin, lower priced competitors when customers came in looking for Apple. The messages by competitors were broad and confusing to the customers so the end result was to reduce the distinguishing points to processor speed and memory size. It was a tough retail environment to be successful in. When you added the amount of software titles to what was being offered by Apple-friendly developers there was a distinct logic to look at Wintel products instead of Apple. In many ways the aspirational aspects of Apple advertising and visibility were driving customers in at the emotional level but losing them on the rational side of the conversation at point of sale. It was a losing proposition for Apple because they had no control. Today, with the exception of most of the automobile industry, most manufacturers control their channel and control the relationship with their customers.

Q: How did you begin the retail design development with Steve?
We were hired personally by Steve to begin the retail program. After reading the white paper and a remarkable interview process, he called us to come in and start creating retail design. My longtime business partner, Wilhelm Oehl, and I worked directly with him by starting with a blank whiteboard creating bubble diagrams in his board room.

Our team at Eight Inc. and the growing Apple retail team and marcom teams met weekly for the better part of 12 years until his time was restricted due to illness. Another Eight Inc. Principal, Matt Judge, worked internally with Apple during the expansion, and our San Francisco studio maintains a team of people supporting Apple's needs to this day. Our team has a long history with Apple and that has led to many other extraordinary business and personal relationships.

Over the years we have evolved a distinct approach and design process to develop new and deeper relationships between companies and people across many business categories; finance, telcos, automotive, hospitality, and airlines have all responded to this approach with unprecedented success. Virgin Atlantic Airways, Citibank, Lincoln China, Citi Private Bank, Coach, Nike, and many other global businesses have benefited from the design of a human-focused experience.

Q: The epitome of retail space design has to be an Apple store. From the materials to the lighting, each has design that shows what the company stands for. The result: the highest-selling spaces on average in the U.S., and perhaps the world. Why is this? Can you explain this for me?

The secrets to Apple's specific success are many. To me, any successful program, including Apple's, is the connection to meaningful value that people feel and understand. Expressing the value proposition through the experience of the brand values is always the focus. Products will come and go but the core brand experience is where the most important aspect of any relationship is built. Trust and values matter ultimately. Those are the attributes that connect people.

When we designed the first Apple store, our challenge was to fill 5,000 square feet and Apple only had four products. Computers occupied the front quarter of the Apple store. The rest of the space was devoted to services (a kids' area, a theater for educational programs, the soon-to-be-signature Genius Bar), software solutions (movies, music, photos), and additional electronics and accessories. All these elements were new ways for people to interact with technology—to extend the ease-of-use approach into a broader dimension rather than just the software interface.

The lighting design, with Sylvia Bistrom at ISP Design, the fabricators and consultants, had to ensure the presentation of the real product would look as good as the lighting used in the Apple communications photography. The design approach was to ensure the product looked as beautiful in real life as the photography but most importantly it was about establishing that sense that what Apple tells you is what they deliver—what Apple tells you about its products can be trusted.

A solution for Apple will be different from Tiffany or Nike or others. As part of that, the experience design should also support the business and reflect its core values. The physical aspects of the program would be created to support those core qualities. It's more about a way of thinking about what you are really trying to accomplish. Yes, retail is commonly measured by transactions. Sales per square foot, etc. But this is the outcome of a number of things that need to work together, and sales are just the result.

The focus is on designing an outcome that connects and generates an emotional connection through distinct experience, building advocacy. It's about designing a distinct experience. It has to begin with offering something relevant that people want but there is much more. Design should either achieve a behavior or create a context for behavior that has a purpose. In our experience human outcomes lead to business outcomes.

Q: What can you tell us about Eight Inc's design of the Apple Stores?
The Apple retail design reflects much of the architectural qualities of the original MacWorld event design concept. The design language was developed to express the brand values. The design of the environment is large scale, simple, and geometric community spaces. Most people experience light, open spaces but the design for the space was to express accessibility and generosity. It was to be: welcoming with broad, open product presentation tables; technologically adept; simple; light; and appealing. A space intended to invite visitors to connect with the brand and the Apple community. The physical design is very well known at this point and has gone through iterations in the first 20 years—today, it's going through its 5th generation now.

In addition to the environments the Apple experience is a function of the products and services, communications and human behavior model. Many companies look to emulate the Apple retail physical look over the years but miss the elements that create a holistic experience. While others look to emulate Apple, we don't see others with the same brand values and attributes, therefore we never believe others should emulate one another. Each company is unique, and Apple and its competitors are no exception. We believe each company should create an experience based on their unique distinguishing qualities and express those clearly for the users or customers to understand.

The design of the Apple stores was intended to convey the things that Apple, its approach to technology and its history had come to represent

—their distinct qualities through the lens of creating great human experience. The openness and accessibility are some things that have been at the core of the company since the beginning. A democratized access to technology is one of the things that moved Apple to create intense customer loyalty—irrational loyalty. People could feel Apple through the journey they were on as technology progressed, and knew Apple was looking out for the human interests along the way. These qualities were important to express in the physical space through many different design elements. Interestingly, during the design process, did it "feel right" often won out over a clear articulation of the conventional retail wisdom. The openness of the space and accessibility was a response to how Steve felt Apple should be perceived—often channeling the qualities without clearly identifying them.

He knew he wanted it to be the most technologicallyadvanced space possible. Alan Moyer who led the initial construction of the retail stores worked closely with suppliers and contractors to build the stores. The glass technology that makes up the stairs, bridges, and in some cases the exterior of the stores, had to be the most advanced. Peter Bohlin and his team, with structural glass innovator James O'Callahan from Eckersly O'Callahan, who created the engineering for the glass system, really pushed the technical capability of the material to do magical things.

When we developed the stainless steel material for the store interiors and exteriors it took us months to design and perfect. It began with the metal panels on the first University Avenue store and became a key part of the Apple design language over time. Only near the end of the development of the material did we understand that acceptance by Steve would come by creating a material solution that others could not or would not emulate easily. The dimension of this was a key part of creating proprietary elements in the design that would distinguish Apple from any competitor.

Shimano Cycling World, Singapore, 2014

Empathy

"Great customer experience is everyone's responsibility and nobody's job."
—Unknown

Shimano Cycling World, Singapore, 2014

Shimano Cycling World, Singapore, 2014

1800s

Shimano Cycling World, Singapore, 2014

Virgin Atlantic Clubhouse, San Francisco, 2000

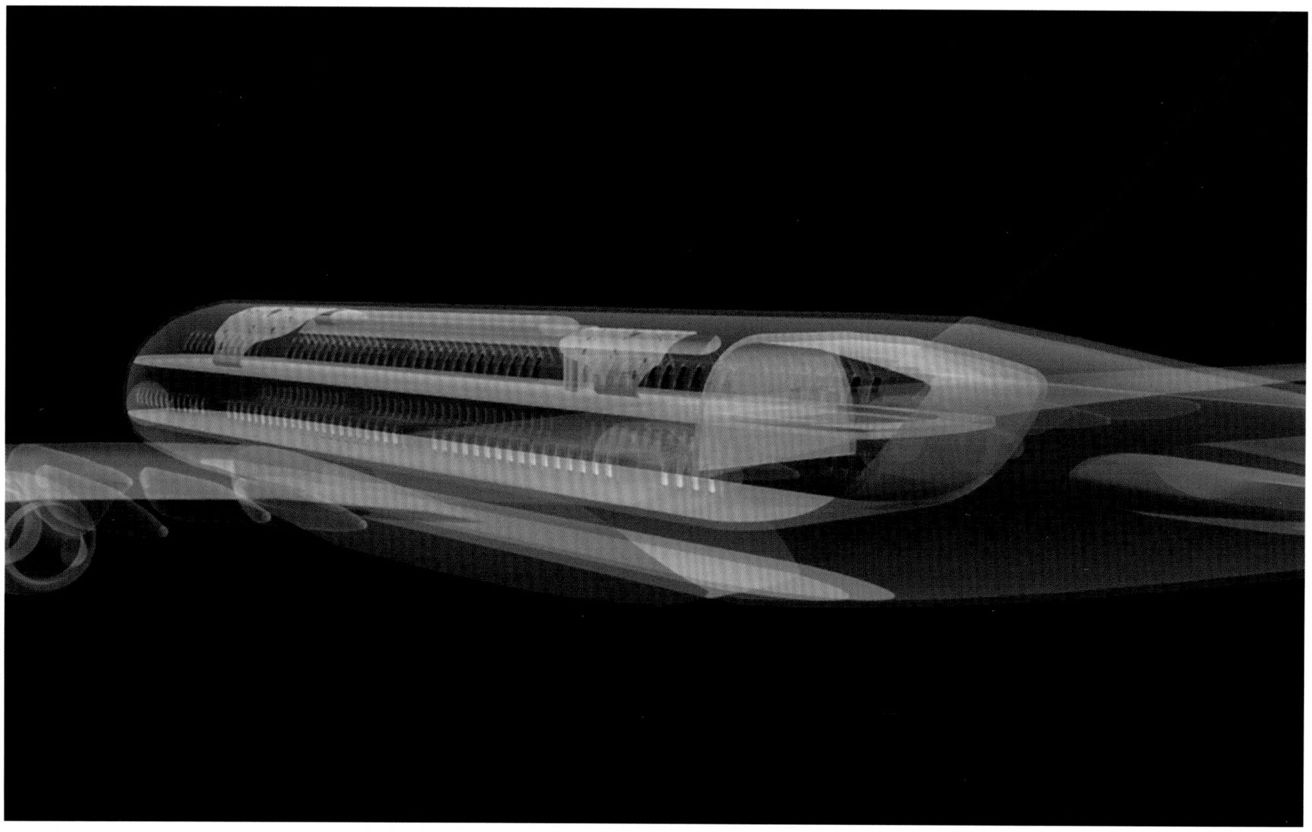

Virgin Atlantic Airline A380, 2006

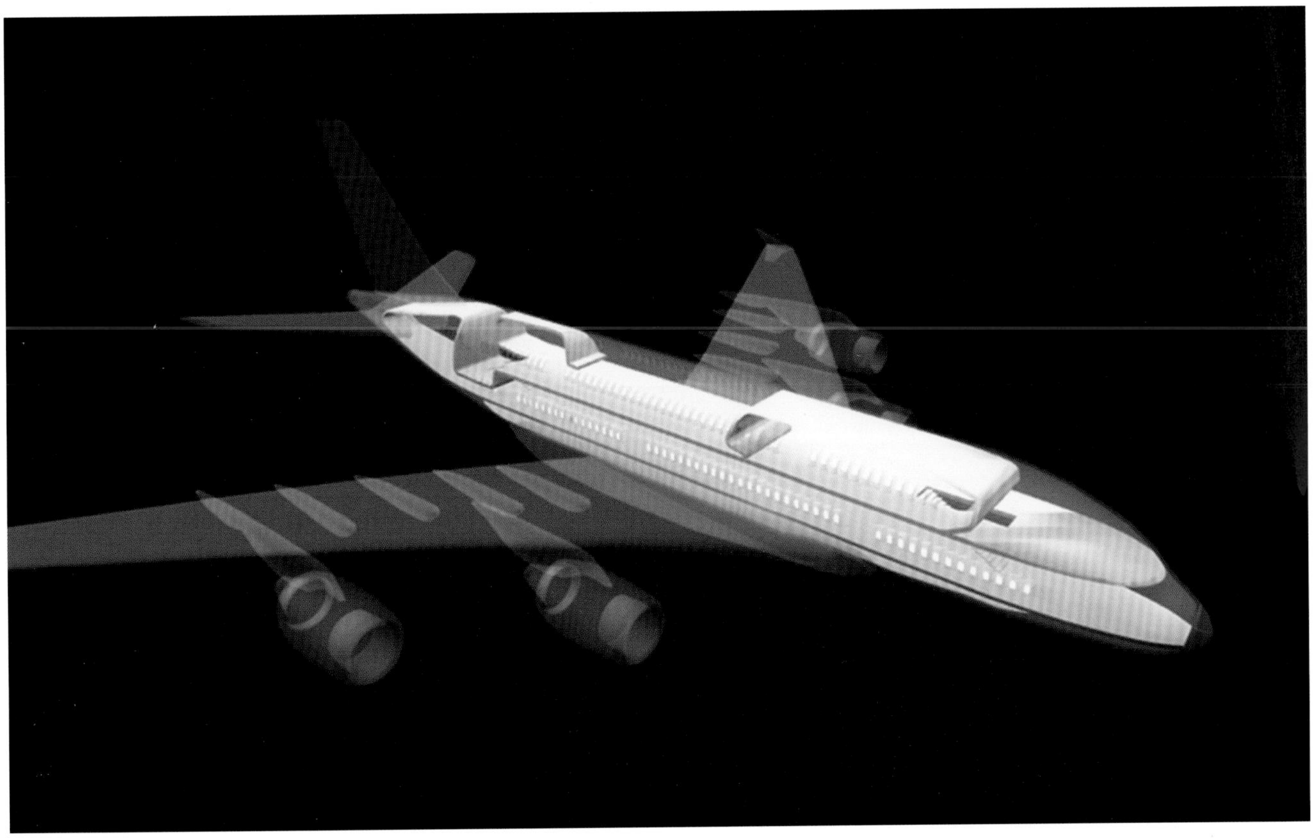

Virgin Atlantic Airline A380, 2006

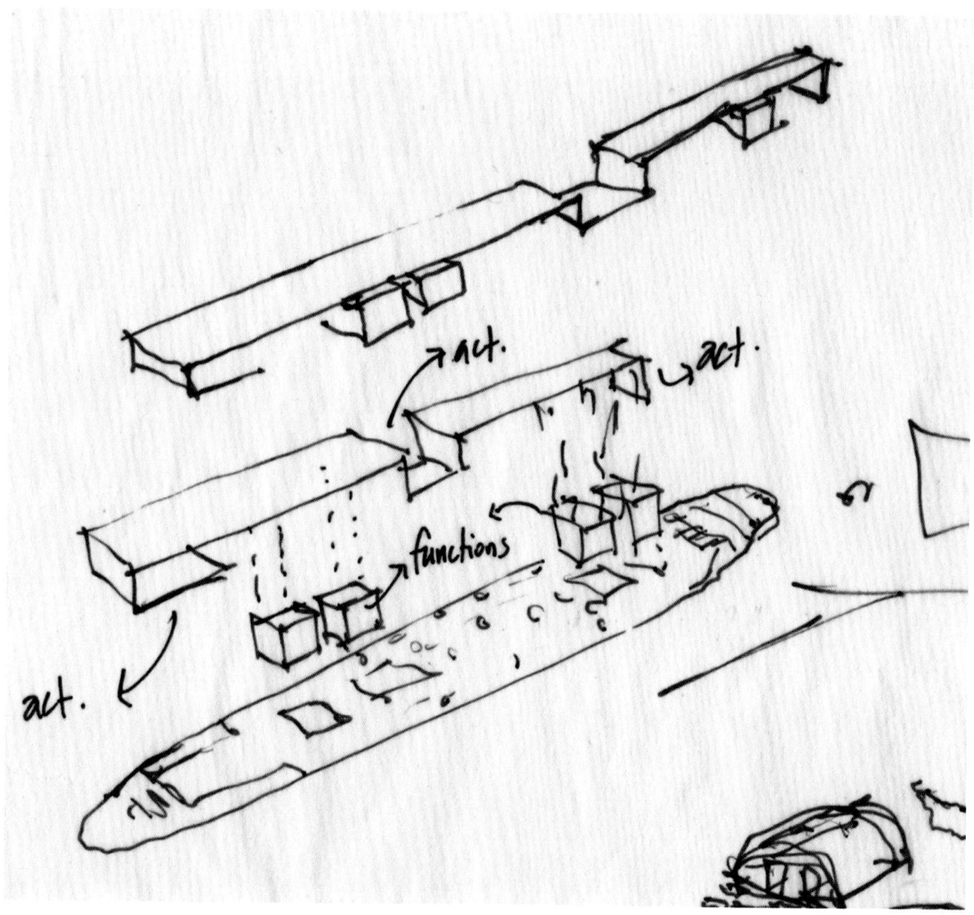

Virgin Atlantic Airline A380, 2006

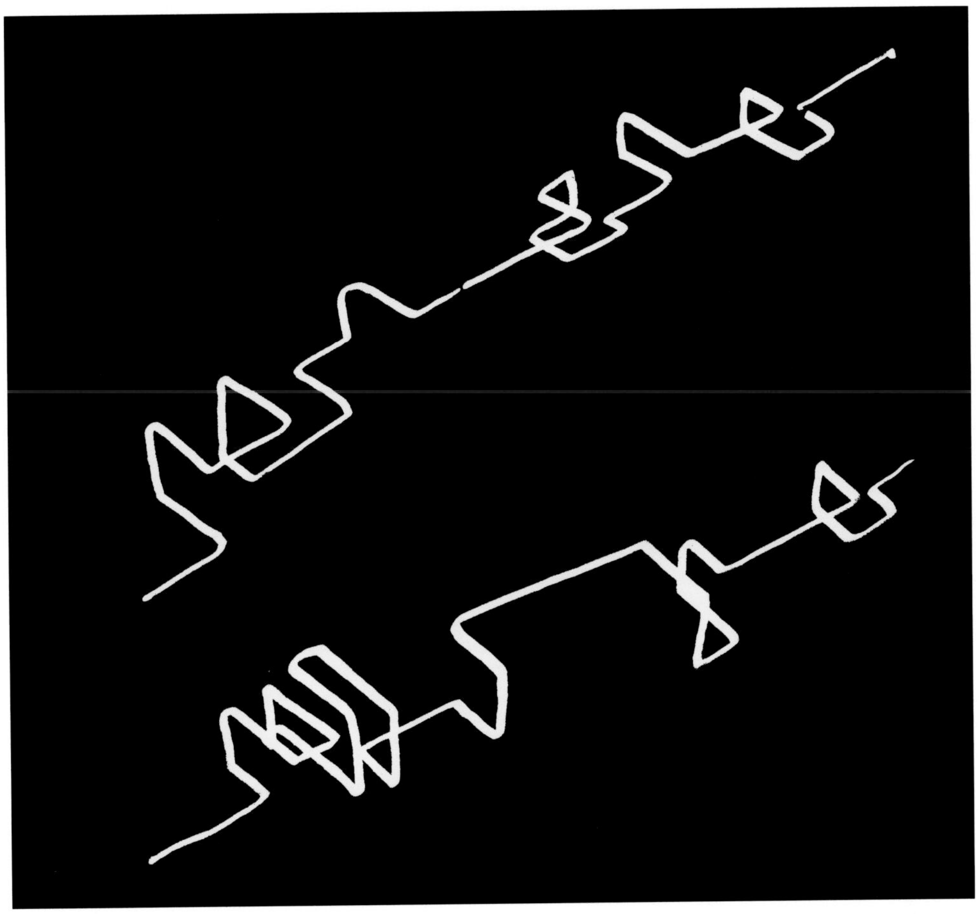

Virgin Atlantic Airline A380, 2006

Virgin Hotel and Casino, Las Vegas, 2006

Virgin Hotel and Casino, Las Vegas, 2006

Virgin Hotel and Casino, Las Vegas, 2006

Virgin Hotel and Casino, Las Vegas, 2006

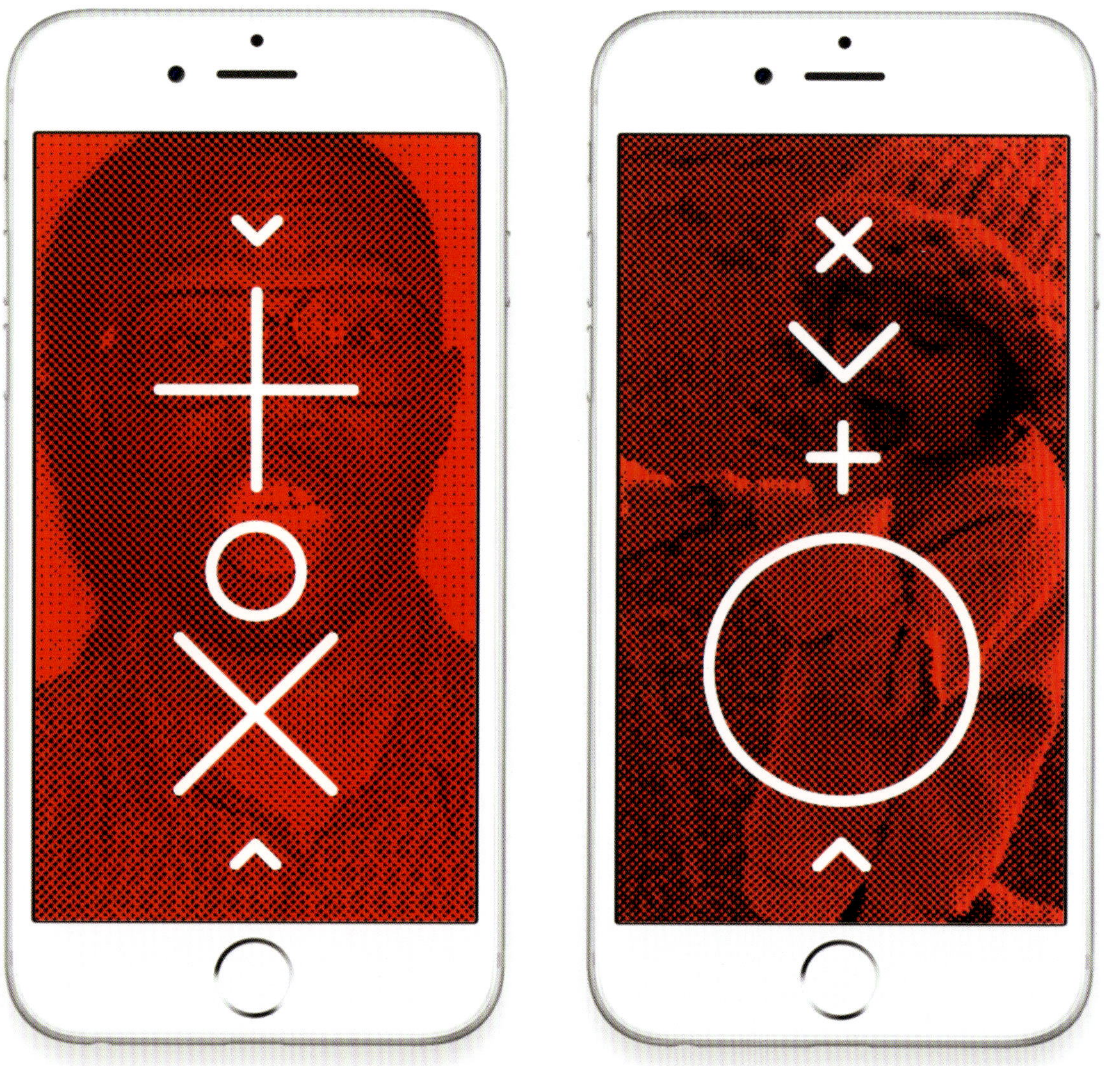

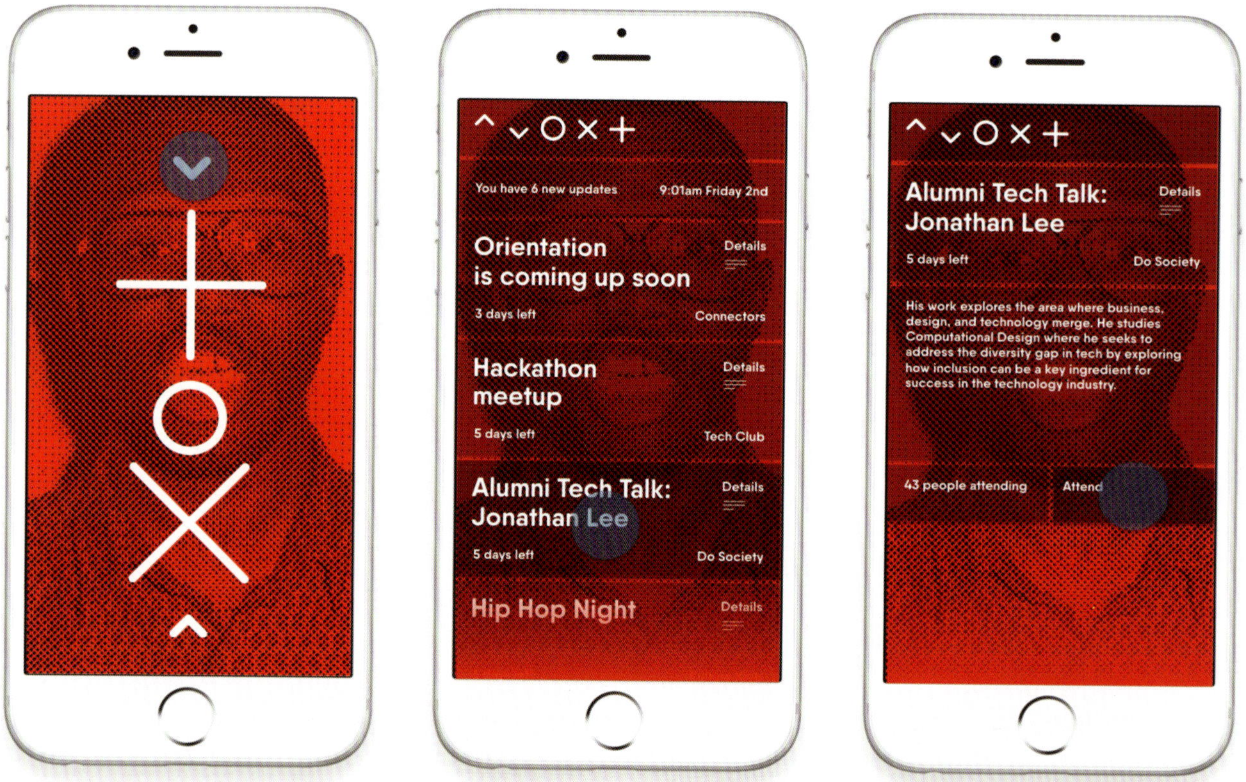

QUT App, Australia, 2016

Q: Why is empathy important in design?

It's not just important in design—it's one of the fundamental qualities that make us successful in any human interaction. Our definition of **empathy** is not to transpose the feelings of others to yourself but to put your perspective of experience through the lens of the people experiencing the product or service.

Empathy. Empathy is an ability that is intuitive and comes naturally for some but may need to be developed in others. It is not how you would feel if you were in the shoes of the "other" but rather the capacity to understand how the other feels in their shoes. All too often we make the false assumption that others' experience is the same as ours or that they will experience what we expect them to experience. It's important that we don't fall into the "assumption trap" whereby we assume that the client or customer will experience what we have intended. To avoid this trap, we must stay open to learning from others and be aware at all times that people can have vastly different experiences that are far removed from what we intended or expected.

There is incredible power in obtaining a better understanding how we live and interact with each other. Ask yourself, how do we fit in with each other and our environment?

Q: What do you mean by empathy?

To focus on better human experience usually means better design. Better design typically leads to better economic or business **outcomes.**

Outcomes. Another way to understand and explain empathy is that it creates a situation in which the client or customer feels "felt" or intuitively understood. The experience of feeling felt establishes a remarkably strong connection between the two parties. The moment we design an experience in which the customer feels felt or intuitively understood we deepen the relationship in a very subtle but powerful way.

To create value, it is essential to better understand the human dynamics and challenges people face. It is impossible for design to be meaningful unless the human outcome is clear. The role of empathy is not to take on the emotion of others but to understand the needs and emotional aspirations of the user, driving connectedness. The best solutions understand both the functional objectives of the user as well as the things the users aspire to. Empathy is possessing a sensitivity to the things that can be improved or changed to make people's lives more successful.

It's about tuning into other people; listening and learning from their behavior, pain points and experiences. It also means we need to have a deeper understanding of human behavior.

Q: Is the ability to fundamentally understand people a unique skill?
Knowledge of human behavior should be fundamental but it's about much **more than knowledge.**

More than knowledge. The development of emotional intelligence starts with self-awareness and the capacity to reflect. As Carl Jung noted, "We can only understand the other person to the extent that we understand ourselves. What we don't know or accept/understand in ourselves, we cannot know or accept in the other". The starting point for deeper understanding of our customers or clients is our self-awareness.

Some call it wisdom but it requires emotional intelligence. Ironically, the value of empathy is less and less understood today, but is critical to successful design.

Empathy is both knowledge and sensitivity. Insights into human behavior, and understanding human psychology, are critical. Experience is based on how people respond to a variety of inputs. There is context to all experience that frames the way we process information. This leads to a competitive advantage in business if it can translate into a better customer experience and create value for people.

Few companies look at the experience as a core attribute of their offerings but that is changing. Gartner research points out customer experience (CX) is the new marketing battlefront. More than two-thirds of marketers responsible said their companies compete mostly on the basis of CX, according to the 2017 Gartner Customer Experience in Marketing Survey. And in two years' time, 81% said they expect to be competing mostly or completely on the basis of CX. This trend has continued as more and more businesses look at how to be more relevant in such a rapidly changing environment.

Most of the time the focus on the user experience make the business more relevant in a market. Great design can make the experience of a place or business into something people desire. In many cases it can help transform companies into leaders. Clearly the desire is to make things better and improve the way people live. This means we must be absolutely relevant in the lives of the people we **serve**.

Serve. And the truth of the matter is that it is not all that easy to ascertain if indeed we are "relevant in the lives of the people we serve". The mistake we make is to assume that we know what is "relevant" in the lives of others... and often we're very wrong. It is only by truly connecting and deeply engaging with others that we can begin to get a sense of what matters to them, what is really important for them and therefore how we can be truly relevant in their lives.

All design is ultimately in the service of others whether that is the initial intent or not. The business outcomes include the **people in the company** as well as those who benefit from the success of the business.

People in the company. The fact that business outcomes include people in the company is an often overlooked aspect. Our focus on the delighting and connecting with customer or client is only as strong as our ability to connect and delight our employees. As Richard Branson noted years ago, we have to treat our employees in the manner we want them to treat our customers or clients. There has to be a consistency in how we treat our employees and how we expect them to engage with our customers or clients.

Q: This leads to how you make things people love?
Passion is an outcome. You need to put the value system of the people you are trying to serve at the front of the priority list. We have to undo the thinking that we were purely architects, interior designers, product designers, and visual communication designers. We have to put aside categorization. Our jobs are not to fulfill a category in a system but to help transform the thinking that has led to some of the biggest success. Our job really is to design things that people feel passionate about. As a design process, that combination of in-depth knowledge of a subject, broad interest, and a persistent curiosity about why or how things became the way they are have always been our strategic advantage.

Q: How does work stay relevant in an era of dramatic change?
In addition to extreme shifts in culture, behavior and the expectations of society, most business categories have never been more at risk, due to disruption by players within and outside their category. Rapid change in the context of a culture or business creates the most risk to a company. Most successful businesses are looking at disrupting their business model before the competition or any outside entity does. I think the ambition often has to be defined as a transformative one; one that reflects a dynamic business world and deeply respects the existing culture.
It's important to keep an eye out for transformation that supports deeper and more meaningful relationships. Our method of interacting has

changed forever with distributed mobile devices, but that is only a step into a larger more profound change.

Q: You often discount the discussion between physical versus digital channels. Why is that?
It is a predictable but meaningless polarity at this point. We are living in Mono-channel or Live-channel world today. We exist in both physical and digital space simultaneously. It was a natural evolution as the mobile channel grew, but the common thread is not the technology or channel. The experience, whether physical or digital, needs to remain a vital one. It connects people and distinguishes the engagements offered.

Today we are engaged in much more diverse methods to accomplish the things we need to do. We often purchase things in the mode we want. For example, that can be in a retail space, collecting products immediately or purchasing for delivery or at a drop station. These are not mutually exclusive but based on the preference of the user at the time. I believe experience has progressed from the omni-channel discussion because of the way digital became a new channel initially to today's Live-channel experience where digital and physical are designed to work together independently and simultaneously.

Q: When you talk about meaningful human outcomes what do you mean?
Meaningful outcomes are the purpose of design. Human outcomes tend to drive successful businesses outcomes. Meaningful human engagement begins with a purpose. Its purpose must serve the needs in absolutely the best way possible. However, the purpose is more than just needs. There are functional ones and aspirational ones. We have to consider the human aspects that make people connect with each other; to design different user journeys to enable functions. Not only to define new ones but to separate the experience from the competitors. It is critical to not only understand the needs and desires but to anticipate the new demands a new experience may produce. Taking new generations into consideration, we find that they are very attuned to whether or not they are genuinely understood, and their values and expectations are taken into consideration. This can only be achieved through the estab-

lishment of a genuinely empathic relationship. Ironically the younger generations are becoming more human as society staggers forward.

Q: You talk about understanding these values as if they are a key influence in design. Why?
It's the starting point. It requires an understanding that all design is dealing with a relationship—a relationship between people who want to connect with other people to provide a product or service. Imagine how difficult it is for people to connect when they do not believe in what the other person believes. As people we connect with other like-minded people. Friends or colleagues bond together over common interests and values. When those values are violated, and trust breaks down, the relationship suffers. Understanding the values of the people you want to connect with and ensuring they align with the values you hold in the company is at the heart of this. It enables a decision-making process to derive the most value for the people you want to connect with. Ironically we are working on ideas and frameworks surrounding Gen Z, the generation that has grown up with technology and sees it as absolutely nothing unique. It's always there and always has been. Much like oxygen.

Q: Understanding the people you want to connect with (customers or users commonly) is the basis but what do you look for?
Most customer research arrives at insights by either quantitative data or qualitative data. Research is often the basis for decisions in most companies, and I would argue research alone. Regardless of the methodology, it can only reflect what we know or what has been. In other words, it's only half of the conversation. It seems absurd but I think half of everything is the past and half of everything is the future. Reliance on research can only give you 48% of the insights you need in design (50% less a margin of error).

Q: How do you achieve a better understanding of what is needed?
Recent research from NYU and Gartner affiliated L2 in New York points to the types of underlying aspects of successful businesses today. Professor Scott Galloway describes a "New Algorithm of Value" where on one axis is the number of "receptors" a business has and on the other axis is the "intelligence" gained and applied to the business.

As an example, when someone searches for something online, Google's search engine gets stronger. This is an incredible and powerful thing. The opposite of a company like Google or Amazon would be magazines where the number of receptors is few and the intelligence gained by the interactions is limited. Hence, relevance is very difficult to derive from the interactions with the products.

There is an increasingly greater need for business to understand more in a rapidly changing time. To develop relevant brand and product experience is critical for success. It's very hard to catch up if you are not engaged in a program that provides those touch points and the analytics to garner value and intelligence to guide the business growth. Shortly after predicting there will be no pure players in retail, either digital or virtual, Amazon acquired Whole Foods. The end of pure-play retail.

Q: Who is able to act on these insights and able to respond with their business in such a rapid manner?
There are the obvious technology leaders. Google, Amazon, Apple and Facebook are among the most valuable companies in the world, and have set various examples of how and where to gather the information. As a result, they have started to separate from the rest of the pack in value but more importantly in information. It's interesting to see what Xiaomi, an electronics manufacturer in China and other companies are doing to harvest the insights from their customers. These businesses are extracting data from having created ecosystems for direct relationships with their customers and deriving incredible information from every interaction. Xiaomi has over a 50 million followers on their social platforms and often publish previews of their next products on these networks. Few companies have a focus group of 50 million people who are passionate about their products. This is a huge advantage in right-sizing the design and supply chain for the business.

The automobile sector is unique. It is one of the few categories of business where most of them do not control the conversation, much less the feedback from their customers. Tesla and others are challenging the lock on dealership networks in the category. What will allow those companies to separate from their competitors are workarounds to the sales touch points. They get feedback in new and creative ways. Once other vehicle makers control the conversation with their customers, the rest of the automobile sector will continue with the traditional dealership model.

Q: Does intelligence derived from interactions seem like a new world version of an old world idea?
It's about dialogue isn't it? But the form has changed. The baker created his products based on a combination of good things he could create and what his customers told him they wanted. If the products were good enough, a customer would buy more and tell others. It was an older and simpler time but the problem today is similar. The competition, timeframe, and responses are much more pressing today. Amazon has brought everything everywhere so now the baker has thousands of competitors in immediate digital proximity. Today we need responsive systems that allow the interactions to be defined by better personalization, and reflect a better connection to the user—systems that strengthen communities of small business and neighborhoods. Imagine a world where the kinds of things you needed were accessible whenever and wherever.

Q: What was the client experience brief for a company like Virgin Atlantic Airways? What was your design response?
Our client who later became a Principal at Eight Inc., Hilary Clark, initially asked for an interior design, "Can you help us design a new lounge?" Virgin had decided their lounges should be distinct from others but were unclear on what that distinction was. Originally, it was not focused on the client experience but the interior design. The vision of each lounge having distinctly different designs was a conscious decision to reflect qualities of an individual market, so that the program was not formulaic in the look and feel of the design. Travelers would know when they were in the New York lounge versus San Francisco or London.

Our initial thought was to look at how lounges fit into the broader travel narrative. What would be distinct in the travel experience? A recognisably Virgin experience? The Virgin clubhouse. We proposed to look at the experience of what people think of traveling from the start until they get to their destination. What are the types of experiences that are relevant to them along that journey? Things that lead to a completely different way of thinking about the facilities and experiences then resulted in the Virgin Clubhouse.

What we brought to the Virgin Atlantic Lounge design was not only a localizing aesthetic but also consideration of how and where the brand values would influence the design of all lounges. We also brought the thought that the lounges were only one part of the user experience broader narrative—in other words, how the lounge would fit into a broader spectrum of the traveler's experience. This is a far more interesting question because it starts to imagine the user experience in a holistic way rather than the lounge being disconnected from the pre-flight experience, the flight experience and the post-flight experience.

Q: Given your experience designing a brand new approach to the airport lounge with your Virgin Atlantic Clubhouse, if you were given carte blanche to re-design the interior of a passenger plane, what would it look like?

When Virgin Atlantic Airways was considering the purchase of the new A380, they commissioned us to take a look at what the Virgin air travel experience could be like on a three-story aluminum tube. The idea of creating a new experience was very exciting to us. We knew the traditional structures could be challenged. The industry standard commoditizes the category.

We would first challenge every assumption that leads to an experience that all other competitors create. The class designation is a holdover from a system of financial class distinction. Why use this? Why not reflect the type of experience based on things you would like to do or accomplish while in transit? Why not create spaces that monetize the experience based on the needs and interests of the traveler? Would you have space to work, rest, or play? Would you express the space and the functions of those primary needs and create a service model that allows for more ways to create value for the traveler that feed directly into the business model of the carrier?

The challenge is always technical concerning flight functionality and the physical limitations of an aircraft. Few start with the experience as a differentiator. Today it is often a capacity factor that is overriding all others and other factors have little impact on the business model. With the fuel prices and growth in air travel, however, there is a space opening up for a new way to travel. The majority of "Economy" flights are arduous at best and likely a health threat some of the time. This category is far behind its potential because most companies express to the traveler that they are a captive audience. It is an area that requires more creative thought to shatter the category norms.

Q: Eight Inc. has had a long history of creating experiences for Virgin? Can you tell us about how you approach design for them?
We chose to define the experience through design. We changed it to be part of the experience a customer has from the moment they think of traveling to when they arrive at their destination and back. It was part of a narrative to start small but think big. There is freedom in the structure and leadership of a company that allows for invention and reinvention. For Virgin, this transformed the way to think about the clubhouse experience and the way to think about their customers. From this, our work over 15 years has been to take a white paper business proposition and bring them to life: Virgin Atlantic Airways lounges, the A380 aircraft experience, Virgin casinos, and hotels. There is a comfort for the absurd as well (one of our studies for the Airbus A380 aircraft interior is a three-level movie theater at the rear of the aircraft). As products and services become more alike, the emotional connection becomes the differentiator. A meaningful experience is one of the best ways to connect on an emotional level.

Q: Is a focus on designing experience worth the cost?
How do you value something that truly matters to people? Its really Return on Experience. Is it transactions? Loyalty? Advocacy? It often defines and creates value if the delivery is through filters that focus on the user experience. If you look at what separates Amazon, Google, Facebook, or Apple, why are these companies worth millions of dollars when they're not the first to market and when they're not necessarily offering the most robust solution or products? They are doing something that connects with people. I think that the design execution is what you are creating and making relevant so that users become your advocates.

> "Fifty percent of the reason people tend to engage with the brand is word of mouth, and direct experience drives 80% of word of mouth" —McKinsey

If you are not focused on designing the experience you are missing out on a tremendous opportunity to leverage value into your company.

Virgin Atlantic Clubhouse, San Francisco, 2000

Creativity

"Making leads to knowing."
—Dr. Lorne M. Buchman
President of Art Center College of Design

EXIT

Virgin Atlantic Clubhouse, San Francisco, 2000

Xiaomi Flagship Store, Shenzhen, 2018

Xiaomi Flagship Store, Shenzhen, 2018

Xiaomi Flagship Store, Shenzhen, 2018

Xiaomi Flagship Store, Shenzhen, 2018

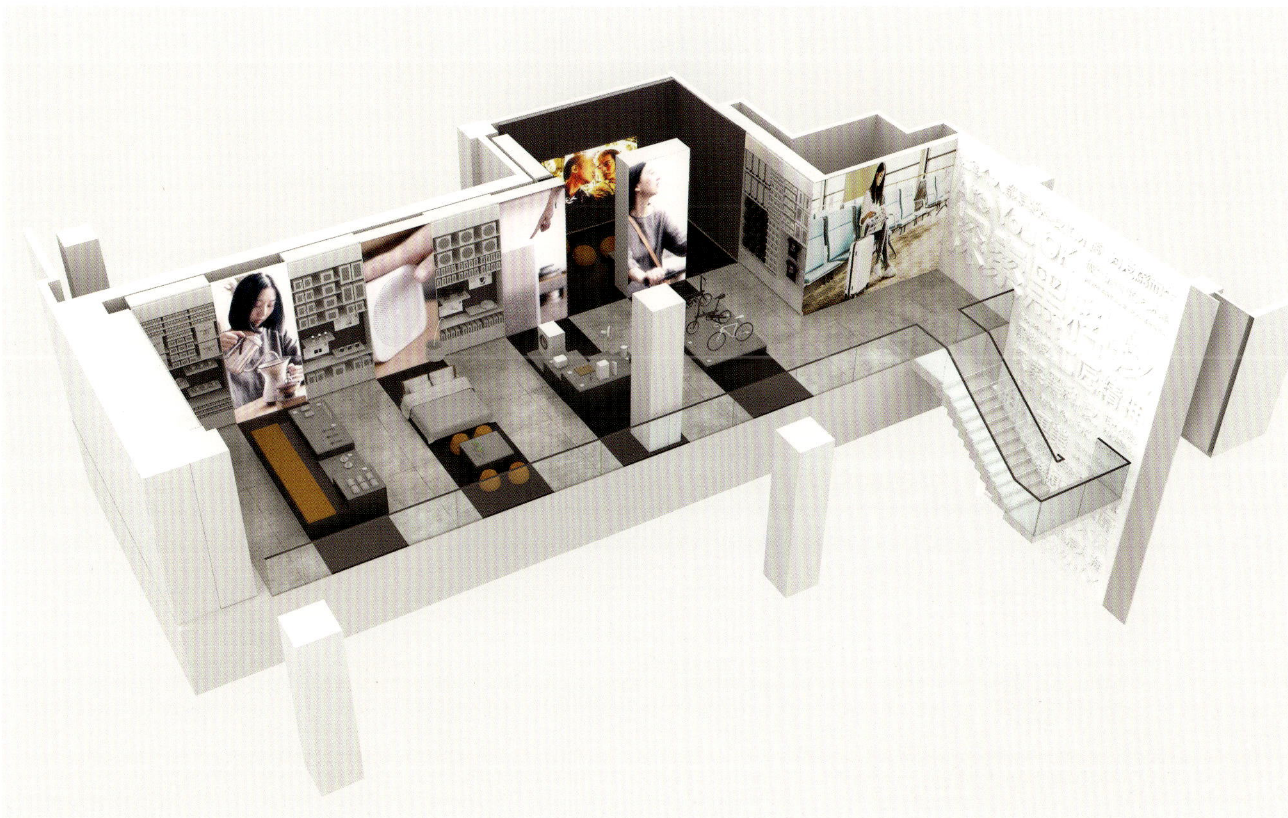

Xiaomi Flagship Store, Shenzhen, 2018

米兔积木机器人
¥499
米兔智能故事机
199

Xiaomi Flagship Store, Shenzhen, 2018

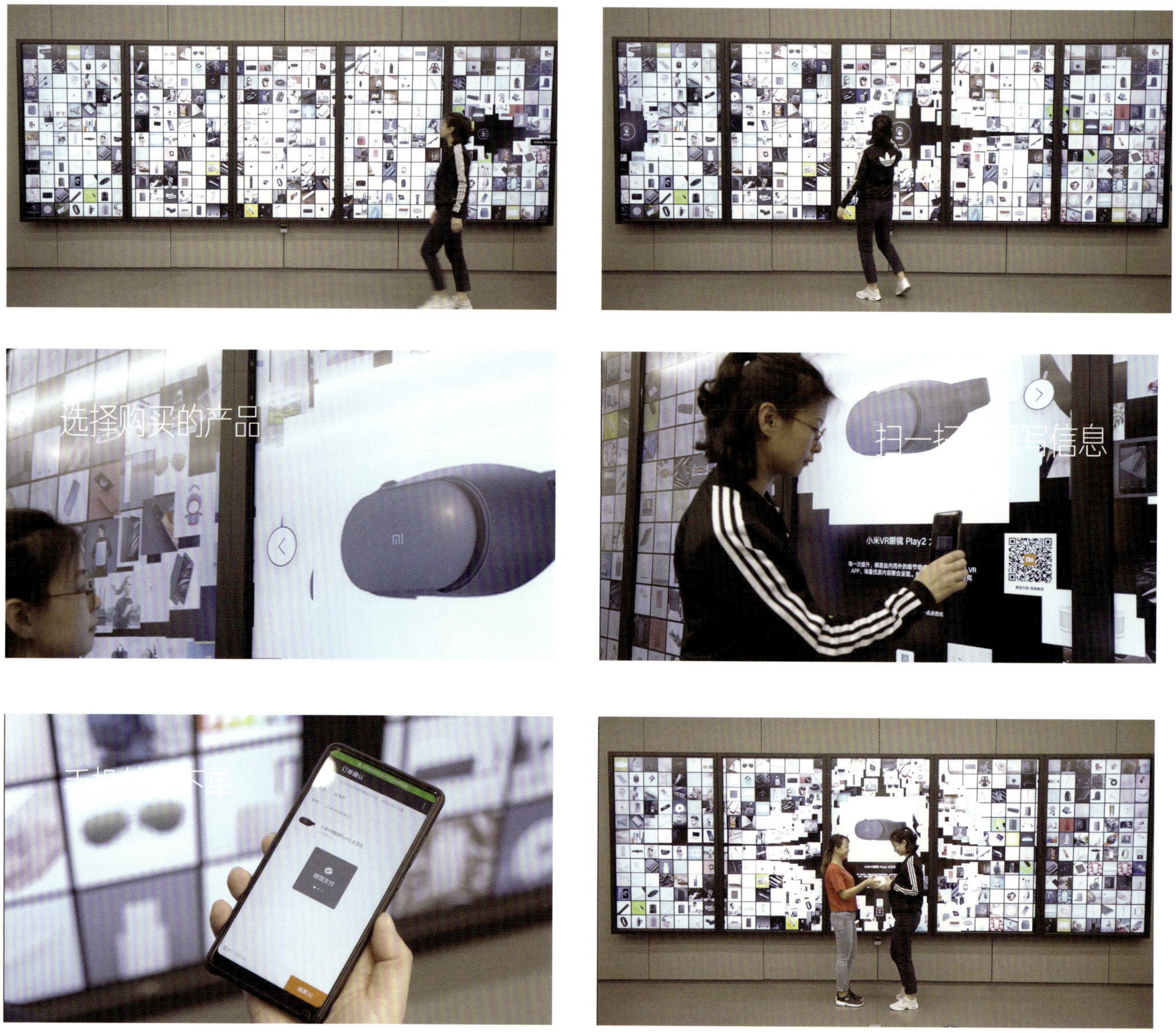

Xiaomi Flagship Store Digital Wall Shopping Experience, Shenzhen, 2018

Xiaomi Flagship Store, Shenzhen, 2018

Xiaomi Flagship Store, Shenzhen, 2018

Xiaomi Flagship Store, Shenzhen, 2018

Xiaomi Flagship Store, Shenzhen, 2018

1

Litro, Romania, 2009

Litro, Romania, 2009

Litro, Romania, 2009

Litro, Romania, 2009

Q: You describe creativity as a business tool?

It is one of the most powerful tools a business can deploy. It is the most important tool any company has, and is maybe the least understood. Most businesses believe optimization and efficient operations of the verticals are the most important. They are critical operationally and look to treat the creative part of the business the same way as the other categories. Most organizations focus on **causal thinking** which of course is necessary but not sufficient to deal with the complexity that executive teams face.

"Making leads to knowing" The key to creativity is to not ask "why?" but rather to explore via "what comes to mind". As the very familiar phrase so aptly puts it, "The answer murders the question."

Causal thinking. The most common question of causal thinking is "Why?" Why did this happen? Let's get to the bottom of things! We need to understand what caused this situation or what we need to do... so think!! However, there is another way of thinking which is referred to as associative thinking. This is the birthplace of creativity as it opens up access to the unknown, the unconscious, and the "yet to be discovered". Associative thinking focuses not on understanding, not on wanting to find solutions but rather on "How can we look at this differently?", "What is it that we are missing, not seeing?" or just simply "What comes to mind?" irrespective of how off-task, silly or just plain preposterous that thought or feeling may seem.

Causal thinking places us in the space of "why?", "how can we understand this better?", "what is the best course of action for us to take?" Associative thinking asks purely "what comes to mind?" It invites the individual or the team to explore perspectives by tuning into their more playful and creative selves which is accessed via the associative thinking mode. Another way of looking at this is that we invite the individual or team to suspend judgment and the wish for immediate answers in order to tune into their unconscious and creative self, which in many cases has been repressed as a result of needing to be "logical" and "rational". While we are not suggesting that one becomes irrational in their approach, we are pleading for the value in suspending judgment and tuning into another way of thinking, represented by the associative methodology. By doing so, one is able to access perspectives, feelings, images and ideas that offer another perspective to sense-making and understanding that otherwise would have remained hidden, buried under the weight of causal thinking.

The associative method also "democratizes" thinking and input within an organization as a contribution from associative thinking that can come from anyone, anywhere within the organization. Indeed, the task of a leader is to be able to engage the entire team or organization in associative thinking so that they can access the greatest volume of creativity, originality and a deeper understanding of the customer experience. We also realize that this is a specific approach that should be followed when the causal methodology is not leading to relevant or actionable results or when the team is stuck. Both modes of thinking are required and essential to team and organizational effectiveness. However, as the default position is to go into causal thinking and to remain there, often turning in circles, the challenge from leadership is to recognize when associative thinking might indeed move the team and creativity further along in the process... and by doing so, to remain open to the "silly, inappropriate, or downright crazy" ideas that surface as a result of associative thinking.

Causal thinking is logical and based on concepts such as root cause analysis. Creativity is extraordinarily valuable in all parts of the human endeavor. In the best companies the leadership understands both modes of thinking.

Building real value comes from the power of unleashing creativity and applying design skill. Most winning companies do this and others could be even more successful with a design focus. Creativity is the real transformative element that drives markets and grows businesses. I see very few businesses that have given up on this and are still healthy. There are two common types of business—ones that create value and ones that extract or destroy value.

Businesses ideally want to try to formalize creativity and be able to manage it the way they do other linear systems in the business. This notion causes a fundamental dilemma. Creativity can be messy and inefficient and sometimes leads to temporary failure. When we worked on the Citi Smart Banking program, the program director was clearly uncomfortable with the non-linear process. "People love great sausage, but don't want to see the sausage making" (Raul Parades, Citibank). This is one reason to build diversity into the team. You need both capabilities of analytics and associative thought. As Picasso once said, "Every child is an artist. **The problem** is staying an artist when you grow up."

The problem. As Nobel Laurate geneticist James D. Watson observed, "people are born curious and then have it pounded out of them." What Tim is focusing on is the importance of reigniting that "spark" of curiosity which has been repressed and ignored in most of us as a result of our educational experiences. Einstein noted that "the only thing that interferes with my learning is my education."

The optimization and management of human resources are best when they are aligned to and support a culture that focuses on creating the space for creativity and design to emerge from a variety of levels.

Q: Can good design transform a business?
Virtually all good design is creative, not destructive. The idea that the creation of value enables business transformation seems natural. The opposite is destruction or dilution of value. The value of strategic design in business is to help you define the next positive change and position

your business in the future you help create. A new idea by definition is "insane".

Q: Would you use creativity as a solution to disruption in business? Creativity is a driver of innovation, but innovation is contextual. The context is often difficult to understand when being disrupted. It requires different thinking. **Experience thinking.**

Experience thinking. Indeed associative thinking is very similar to what Tim refers to as experience thinking because the focus on the experience of the other leads to ideas, suggestions, perspectives and new ways of understanding the known reality that is beginning to emerge. One could say that the consequence of tapping into the unknown connections, feelings, perceptions and ideas that have been garnered as a result of the associative experience enables the individual or team to harvest what one might call "the un-thought known" (Bollas, *The Shadow of the Object: Psychoanalysis and the Unthought Known,* 1987).

It requires diversity. There are many clues that business is becoming stale and at risk of disruption. The natural tendency is to coast when you can. Hey, business is not that bad, and we are growing. Let's not tip the scales. The problem is that it is probably the time to be looking into how you can disrupt your business and operating model. You have cash and investing in the future is far more comfortable without the pressure of survival breathing down your neck. Once you have gotten ahead, sitting back gives your competitors a chance to catch up. We often see clients struggle with this as they fear the disruption of change to their current success. However, holding on to the status quo is a sure way to ensure failure as the customer continues to evolve and eventually feels disconnected from your product or service. Each business sector should be identifying risk space and feeding it to the **innovation team.**

Innovation team. I would make the point here that not only should each sector identify the risk space and feed its findings to the innovation team but they should also share the creative new space that only they can identify due to their deep knowledge and experience with the customer or consumer. This means that innovation and creativity have to come from throughout the organization. While this is not a new thought, it is surprisingly difficult for most leaders to actively embed such a practice in their teams and organizations. In doing so it is possible to create a very different team and organizational culture... one in which creative and new ideas or ways of doing things can emerge from anywhere in the organization. Clearly not all ideas are equal but many of the ideas that emerge might, based on further elaboration and fine-tuning, open up a new perspective, a new business, a new approach, or a new way of doing things or of surprising the client/customer.

I can't emphasize this point enough. Tim addresses the importance of the relationship. Most companies fail to establish a true relationship with their customers. The distinction between relationship and relatedness made earlier is crucial here. The relationship is based on an emotional connection and shared values, meaning, experiences, etc. It is a wish to be genuinely connected to the customer. Relatedness is more instrumental and transactional, and is based on assumptions and not on actually connecting and interacting with the other person(s). Businesses that are able to establish a relationship do so by connecting at a personal level. The customers feel understood, valued and appreciated. Businesses that fail to establish a relationship based on relatedness are at risk of completely misreading the customer's perspective and are in fact often experienced as being completely out of sync, indifferent, disinterested or even hostile towards the customer's experience and perspective.

Q: You have been working in financial services for a number of years. What are the challenges in changing a conservative category such as banking?

We initially began with a program for Citibank with Jonathan Larsen and the Citi Ventures team with Chris Kay and Debby Hopkins. We created their "Smart Banking" program followed by Citigold and their Private Bank Experiences in London, Singapore and New York. Other engagements with Maybank in Malaysia, CMB in China, Barclays in London and a recently completed transformation program for Akbank in Turkey have been incredible opportunities to help an industry in transition. Ultimately it is to offer relevance to a service category being radically altered by technology and behavior. To define what insights and capabilities a bank (or what used to be a bank) would possess today. Transactions are commoditized, so you need to look at what will uniquely position the company within the market as the go-to authority for growth and business insights that lead to financial success. The ambition has to be a transformative one; one that reflects a dynamic culture, and that supports a more partnered meaningful relationship. The few remaining banks, where arrogance dominates the experience, are effectively walking dead.

Meaningful engagement begins with the recognition of relationship and purpose. Its purpose is to serve the customer's needs in the best way possible. They have to recognize diverse tasks to enable traditional banking functions and define new ones that separate them from the competitors. As transactions move more and more to mobile devices, the physical space needs to become one of the vital places to connect people and to distinguish the services that a "bank" can offer.

This means providing the place and the expertise for people who are imagining a new business, who are looking to grow their family or to grow their wealth. The new bank is not a bank anymore. It is more a place to help people create the future they desire. It's not the *pipes* but the *aspiration* that a financial partner can help deliver. The position helps transform people's dreams into successful realities.

To create a new future will require a new experience. It will take money, and it will require insights that can't be found in a Google search. There are plenty of reasons existing banks have a competitive advantage over NewCo's. Banks are in a unique position to leverage access to insight, successful prior outcomes, deeper network connections and financial capabilities. Others are coming on fast however. The ease and speed of Tencent or Alibaba to convert to a relevant financial services provider, particularly focused on transactions is significant. The opportunity to create new products and services will be found through interactions and feedback; in helping to develop people's futures, rather than insights, through transactions.

Q: Does creativity create value?
If managed well, a leading creative team can make the company relevant and more valuable. Creativity is a key to creating value and can enhance differentiation. Differentiation is essential in a competitive marketplace. A lack of differentiated experience leads to parity. Parity leads to commoditization. Unless you want your business to be perceived as all of the other competitors in the category, the market will force you to distinguish yourself.

There is a **common misconception** that because best practices work in creating operational efficiencies that the same applies to creating branded experiences.

Common misconception. I would like to reinforce Tim's comment about "best practices at work" as best practices are in and of themselves based on causal thinking. In fact the moment we ask people to just follow best practices we are explicitly telling them to "stop thinking". I'm not suggesting that best practices are not necessary in order to create standards and efficiencies but we need to be very, very careful in terms of when and how we apply best practices as they do not permit questioning or exploring other ways of approaching a situation. Part of the problem with best practices is that they are based on history. They are based on what worked in the past and therefore, by definition, they do not focus on "what could we do differently?" Or, "how else could we approach this?" There is little learning in the application of best practice and often creative ideas are experienced as a threat or risk by those who champion "best practice".

In fact, the most successful companies are those who offer a distinct brand experience, deliver on it reliably, and build an irrationally loyal customer base. If you look for best practices, it allows you to be in the game but not a leader when it comes to the user or customer experience.

A successful application of a creative team can obviously drive innovation and a become one of the tools to create distinctive experience. But design is contextual. It requires diversity. Many people say you need a vibrant artistic environment for creativity to be successful. It is an advantage, but I would argue that you need a design ecosystem that provides for the most **significant ideas** to become a reality for most people.

Significant ideas. The concept of psychological safety is essential in terms of creating the space and opportunity for those significant ideas to become reality. The creation of psychological safety within a team or an organization is explictly the task of the leader. It means that any and all opinions are welcome and will be openly explored and considered. Everyone feels safe to express any and all ideas, no matter how "crazy" or "off the wall" these ideas may seem. It is about creating the space and conditions where people can explore these ideas and disagree without concern for being negatively sanctioned in one way or another.

> "People are born creative and then spend a lifetime having it beaten out of them" —Sir Ken Robinson.

Places like Beijing may be noted for a vibrant artistic economy, but the balance of the ecosystem of creativity translating into unique and original business successes are still emerging. Xiao Guan Tea and others are breaking out of the business as usual approach and leveraging creativity. While there may be a need for a "vibrant artistic environment," the idea that this is necessary for innovation to take place immediately excludes those who are nearest and closest to the customer. Those who have the most interactions with the customer should also be involved in the exploration of the positive benefit for the customer.

Some places are able to combine the best resources to deliver innovation. Those places, such as Silicon Valley, Singapore, or Tel Aviv, where there is a balance of business, creativity, capital, and energy, can provide a far more powerful environment for improving people and intimately supporting successful business outcomes. Again, balance and diversity is a competitive advantage.

Q: What kind of influence does design have on our perceptions?
Regarding influence, the design is often the thing that defines those who stand out when competing in a highly competitive environment. Design affects how a brand is perceived and what value it possesses. When products move beyond a commodity, design is a crucial differentiator.

Q: Does design influence success?
More than influence, the design is often the thing that defines the winners when the business is in a highly competitive environment.That said, a company is defined by the products and services it offers combined with the experience that users have with those products and services. Experience design recognizes a key factor influencing **adoption and integration**.

Adoption and integration. In terms of the key factors influencing successful adoption integration being the human experience, I think there are several factors. In order for adoption integration to be successful, there is a need to connect not only at the rational (causal) level but, much more importantly, to be able to engage others at a level that resonates with the deeper, nonlogical, non-rational aspects that reside within all those involved. This tends to be much more intuitive and also much more closely aligned to the associative approach. It's the moment where we as the customer think to ourselves "how did they know I wanted this?" or "how did they figure out that this was exactly the issue that I was struggling to resolve or hoped to find an answer to?"

However, there is another factor at play here and this is related to the concept of primary task and primary risk. We can relatively easily state that the primary task of all organizations operating in the retail space is to be seen by the customers as adding value. While one might think that profit is the primary task, profit is a result of the value that an organization delivers to its customers. Indeed, all too often a company loses sight of this distinction and finds itself focusing on profit at the expense of their "value add" contribution, which always leads ultimately to value destruction and a disconnect from the customer.

However, there is a second factor at play as well and that is the primary risk. The primary risk can be defined as the risk of choosing the wrong task (Hirshhorn, 1999 & Krantz, 2010). There are many ways in which one can be perceived as value adding by the customer. The primary risk for any organization is the risk of choosing the wrong task. For example, at one point in Apple's early history they were faced with the decision around whether they were going to have a mass market product focus or an innovation leader focus. Both were viable options but it's very difficult to deliver both equally well. Ultimately, the decision was made for the innovation leader focus... and, as they say, "the rest is history". I think it is safe to assume that if they had chosen for the mass market option, Apple would be in a much different and less successful position today.

The primary risk was very clearly represented in the choice that they had to make. This dilemma—the choice of the correct primary task and the associated primary risk—plays an enormous role in the domain of innovation. It requires constantly challenging the current state of the organization and the current "value add". Working at an unconscious level, the primary task and primary risk, play a most significant role in decision making. Even "rational decisions" have an irrational component and are influenced greatly by the unknown and unacknowledged factors such as the primary risk.

The role of the leader is to be able to identify the primary risks associated with the innovation being proposed as this will greatly impact the successful adoption and change necessary to implement the new idea or product. Failure to identify and acknowledge as well as address the Primary Risk is one of the key factors in failure to successfully innovate and change.

In the absence of an acknowledgement of the Primary Risk and an awareness of how this risk can be addressed and contained, the team or organization will create structures and processes in order to help them contain and avoid their anxiety and uncertainity. These "solutions" are always suboptimal if not counterproductive, as their focus is no longer on the innovation or primary task but rather on containing the anxiety associated with the primary risk.

Eight Inc. Hong Kong Principal, Chris Dobson defines successful experience as "consistent threads that drive human behavior based on the way we are wired, whether psychological or biological, and we respond in similar ways when the interactions are meaningful and add value."

This is the list of things that are the Eight Inc. universal experience factors that drive successful human outcomes:

1. Through its actions and behaviors, address a basic human need.
2. Be designed as a direct expression of the purpose, vision and values of the business or brand staging it.
3. Be simple to locate, access, navigate and interact with.
4. Technology within it should enhance or simplify the human experience. It should never insist upon its presence.
5. Effectively use receptors and intelligence to create progressive human value over time.
6. Be enhanced by the human interactions with it.
7. Be a part of or a start of an ongoing dialogue with the brand or business staging it.
8. Enhance the product or service ownership experience or brand relationship.

With any human experience, there are people, activities, and context. It is the combination of these three that define the experience. If you can create a positive outcome from the design through experience, this often separates winning companies from their competitors.

Q: Why have many companies overlooked customer experience?
First companies have to believe it is important. It's also difficult to do well. Many companies focus on tactical improvements based on increased efficiency and lower operational costs. Not surprising, but this approach is the baseline for a company. The focus has moved away from the customer experience because of the belief that price and schedule is a primary decision factor over experience. The "standardization" of the experience creates operational efficiency. Few of the business decisions are based on creating a distinctive brand experience. Great experience design creates a distinct experience for the user or customer that helps separate the company in a crowded field. This experience is a different experience in its category and a relatively true and undoubtedly preferred customer experience.

Q: How are customers' relationships changing when it comes to brands or companies?
The idea of deepening the relationship with the customers begins with providing more meaning. Aspects of the experience are very much rooted in preferences; if you look at most experiences people have, it's a customer-driven set of choices. Right now, it's an industry driven set of favorites and there's a dynamic there that is shifting. Technology can help enable people to control those things so that the results are robust. Preference can also be a trap to resist the new. Who knew we had preferences for interactions before the iPhone? No one. Preference is a contextual view—looking at what is. It is always critical to look at what can be as well.

Globe Live, Manilla, 2018

Differentiation

**"80% of CEOs believe they're offering a differentiated product, while only 8% of consumers believe those same companies are offering a differentiated product."
—Bain & Company**

Globe Live, Manilla, 2018

Globe Gen3 Retail, Manilla, 2018

Globe Live, Manilla, 2018

Caffè Sienna
Jurlique
Glue

Chapel Street Plaza, Melbourne, 2020

Chapel Street Plaza, Melbourne, 2020

Chapel Street Plaza, Melbourne, 2020

LINCOLN

Lincoln, China, 2015

Lincoln, China, 2015

Lincoln, China, 2015

王顺明/武夷大红袍
WUYI DAHONGPAO

Xiao Guan Tea Retail Store, Jinan, China, 2016

贵客到
小罐茶
8位制茶大师作品
XIAO
GUAN
CHA
小罐茶

Xiao Guan Tea Retail Store, Jinan, China, 2016

Q: You describe differentiation as a competitive advantage. Why is differentiation important?
Differentiation is one of the most important aspects to consider in a competitive environment. Any touchpoint is a point of customer interaction. Differentiation is one of the essential elements to identify and amplify the business value proposition. It is the opportunity to separate a business from its competitors. Differentiation is necessary for a competitive market. A lack of differentiated experience leads to parity.

When you create a new company, you often look at your peer companies in a category and seek to establish yourself by belonging to the group. It seems natural and comforting to fit in but it's an incredible business risk. As a leader, you want to separate from your competitors and elevate what makes you distinct. You never want to be perceived as all of the other competitors in your category. There is a common misconception that because best practices work in creating operational efficiencies that the same applies when creating branded experiences.

Even when a company develops something distinctive, it often offers that product or service in the same way as it always has and the same way competitors do. It is one of the most common traits of a new category of business wanting to be part of the competition. Unfortunately, established businesses continue with the same approach that got them into the game and behave like an entry brand by emulating the others. The result is that they lose much of the advantage that they should have gained.

Emulation = Parity and Parity = Commoditization.

Q: What is a key to differentiation?
If you are looking at your peers it's a good indication you will make similar decisions as your competitors and fall into the same solutions. Design is a powerful tool in creating differentiation in a competitive context, and yet it is often unclear how to convert the skill into successful human outcomes. Successful brands are distinctive. To achieve differentiation, something new has to be created. Creativity fuels originality. When Ron Johnson named the Apple Genius Bar it could have been called a service counter, and no one would have cared. By defining the Genius Bar experience, creating a proprietary name, we had a unique, distinctive experience. The exclusive identity becomes the words for people to use when describing what is unique. The Genius Bar was not only a distinctive experience, it gave Apple guests a key talking point. It helped drive the core brand experience to a new level. The **things people share** about an experience become critical to the conversation. The proprietary terms we create to communicate the experience are a valuable component of any distinctive experience.

Things people share. Crucial here is the dynamic of a shared experience identity that sets us apart. We are different, and we share and cherish that difference. This contributes deeply to the "irrational loyalty" that Tim refers to. It actually is not irrational but rather it is not commonly understood. If we look below the surface we can see that the "irrational loyalty" can actually be understood as an aspect of belonging to a special group and being identified with that special group in a manner that reinforces our wish not only to be different but special. As a result, many people wish to join that "club". Often this process takes place outside of our conscious awareness. For the most part, we don't consciously say to ourselves: "I like how I feel when I enter this store. I can identify with the product and the staff who live those values. Because of this, I would prefer to identify with the company and its products and will purchase from them." But this is exactly what happens when we experience a stong positive resonance with a company's brand and its products.

Q: Why focus on experience?
It reframes the priorities of any design. Any successful business needs to be focused on its customers to remain successful and retain a competitive advantage. It shifts to a focus on human needs and desires. It defines real value. For the experience to be successful it should be created through a focus on the human benefits and outcomes. Creating value is the objective. Whether it is to lead or to survive, the intentional framing of experience will drive value if done properly. It is a way to be meaningful to those people you want to value what you offer. Design-led companies today are the most successful, but it is typically not

recognized or elevated in the business organization structure. Creative thinkers are difficult to manage with linear thinking as a dominant aspect of business education. It's ironic as I believe this is a great place to explore for competitive **advantages.**

Advantages. As mentioned in the book *The Innovators DNA* (Dyer, Gregersen, Christensen, 2011) innovation requires both the discovery as well as the delivery component in order to successfully achieve that innovation. One of the difficulties however is that those who are strong in discovery typically tend to become quite frustrated with those who are strong in delivery and vice versa. The competitive advantage that Tim speaks of is the condition when an organization is able to appreciate and integrate both the discovery and delivery aspects so that they are able to work together in order to bring the innovation to life. As Tim has mentioned on several occasions, one of the unique talents that Steve Jobs possessed was to be able to integrate both his discovery and his delivery perspective at appropriate times in order to drive the innovation within Apple that was also aligned with the customers' expectations. This is true for many of the CEOs of leading innovative companies.

Eight Inc.'s North American President Matt Judge defines experiences as "our emotional responses to moments in our lives. They can be shared but are rarely identical. In fact, they are entirely personal—shaped by the nuances in our belief systems (which in turn, to complicate matters, are shaped by our experiences), which means, at their most granular level, no two experiences are the same."

Q: Can you differentiate through experience?

Touchpoints communicate. They may be the best way to connect companies to others. The experiences people have with companies are formed by a combination of the interactions they have. Those are the things that connect users or customers with your company. **Touchpoints** are one of the key tools to express what makes a business unique from its competitors.

Touchpoints. An important factor here is that the "touchpoints" have to be experienced and based on a genuine sense of relationship rather than an artificial connection based exclusively on commercial interest. If the experience is purely based on a commercial exchange, we may feel pleased with the purchase but we will not experience the "irrational loyalty" that comes when there is a deeper connection and identification with the brand and product. There has to be a sense of connection between the company and the customer so that there is a sense of shared experience. This results in the loyalty and passion for the brand that Tim refers to as well as to the willingness of customers to forgive mistakes because there is a sense of genuine trust and relationship based on that "irrational loyalty".

Ensuring customer experience alone is not the only tool for success. Without great product, it is impossible to truly leverage what a great brand experience can give you concerning in terms of value.

Q: How does experience design work?
The key is understanding that all touchpoints a company offers are an integral part of the relationship. Among people, companies, or individuals, experience is fundamentally based on a relationship. This relationship is based on shared values. It is a common understanding and a guiding philosophical center. To make the relationship strong and compelling, we look at experience touchpoints as the critical ways to communicate those shared values. At the heart of this are the people you are looking to connect. It's a decision-making process to derive the best possible engagement for them with the company or brand. It should be focused on **things that matter** to the people who purchase or participate in the business.

Things that matter. It may seem obvious to point this out but there has to be a genuine desire on the part of the company to connect with their customers beyond just "getting the sale" and that is the larger shared experience that goes beyond the sale to incorporates an emotional and philosophical grounding shared by both parties. This is indeed the holistic human experience that Tim is referring to, and it links back to the concept of "irrational loyalty" and helps us understand how that happens.

Human experience is holistic. We need to frame the design then to support the primary elements that make up a holistic experience. Why hire an architect or designer of a particular core competency without understanding the holistic objective for the experience. These elements are considered in a holistic way and are the parts of any successful relationship. This diagram represents our approach to creating successful experience architecture. This is why we created an **Experience Master Plan**. It is something that creates the necessary framework to translate the values of a company into experience principals and guides the decisions a company makes in any category to align with the intended human outcomes.

Eight Inc. Experience Realms, Copyright 2005

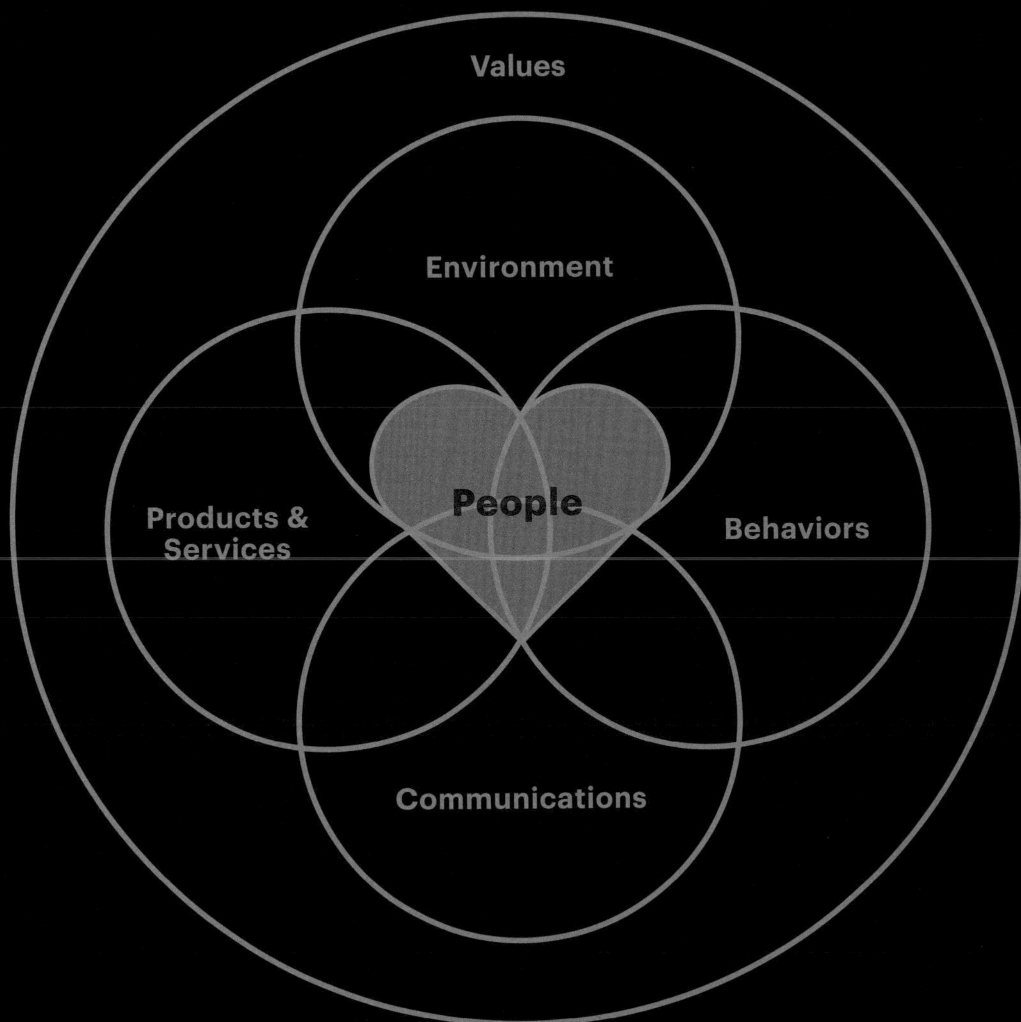

Eight Inc. Experience Realms
Our experience realms recognize that people experience things holistically. Each realm contributes to the overall experience that connects the values of a company with those of the people they wish to connect with. Experience outcomes are more than the sum of these parts.

Q: You say design should be holistic. What do you mean?
With a focus on experience, it is critical to understand people. People experience things in a holistic way. This is a natural human condition. To design an experience by focusing on the part of the component is unnatural. It is not how our perceptions or emotional responses are typically engaged. To look at a solution through a holistic lens is a kind of result of reverse engineering or outcome.

Experience is holistic. We see things in a context, with a combination of influencing factors. Experience is typically a product of people, activities, and the meaning of that activity. A holistic experience is a combination of four primary realms: the environment of the human activity; the communications; the products or services; and the behavior. These four realms make up the primary way to understand the experience. They are interrelated and if done well can support an intentional outcome. All design is understood by the outcomes or the purpose of what is being created.

The best design is a design that looks at a problem from an experience perspective, not by categories or by disciplines. Those operating in a category or specific design discipline can contribute to success, but without a proper experience framework or Experience Master Plan the ability to gauge whether the results have merit becomes challenged. The tools to evaluate the organization must be within the outcome that identifies as relevant to the company. This approach has worked for us for nearly three decades as we've applied it to business categories from consumer electronics, to finance, hospitality, automotive, airlines, education, and healthcare.

Q: How do you approach creativity when you have a clear understanding of the consumer?
Patrick Cox, Eight Inc. Chief Innovation Officer, says, "You don't design for narrow roles like users or consumers. People are far more interesting and complex than that. You don't design in artificial disciplines, or think purely digital or physical, because the reality is more fluid and interconnected than that." Some consultants tend to focus on parts and often risk the outcome by not delivering the experience in line with a clear holistic

strategy. Organizations are not typically structured to accept lateral thinking. It's ideal when we engage from the beginning to the final creation of the experience; an approach that begins with a strategic or transformational initial phase, through the creation or design stage to the implementation or production phase. This is an end-to-end process, designed to deliver the ideal outcome and ideal design experience. The initial steps in a design process consist of creating knowledge and insights that are not not necessarily framed around the typical business objectives necessarily. We would start by understanding why a company has value and a reason to exist in a market. What is the fundamental purpose and how can people extract meaning?

Q: Describe Experience Design?
A way to create effective relationships. An approach to design. A focus on human outcomes. A parallel way of thinking about interactions people have with a company. Experience design is the focus of the human outcome from some form of interaction or activity. The term is commonly used in the digital space, but it pertains to all design. It can be spatial, digital, or any combination of forms that lead to a connection. It is typically not singular and usually more valuable. It concerns outcomes for people in ways that affect behavior and meaning.

Joseph Pine II, the author of the *Experience Economy,* wrote about the progression of economic value. In his book he describes the progress of economies, how we move from merely providing goods or services to an economic ladder that layers experience and transformation as progression beyond the basic economy of goods and services. For us, one of the exciting parts of his work is the idea that the next competitive battleground lies in the staging of experiences, and the next level above that will be guiding the human transformation. Without approaching any design problem from the human experience perspective, you risk missing something in your solution.

Q: Is experience design important for a company?
Design is generally not well understood, and is managed in the way as other teams are in a business. Many of the large, old-world businesses today are buying up design firms at a rapid rate. It will be interesting to see if those same companies can extract value from those teams. It is critical that these companies know how to convert creativity to value or the creative teams they have built will ultimately become expendable when accounting looks to justify their existence. In *Collective Genius*, Linda Hill, Greg Brandeau, Emily Truelove, and Kent Linebacker extract lessons from the companies that seem to extract value from their creative teams consistently. "The rhetoric of innovation is often about fun and creativity, but the reality is that innovation can be very taxing and uncomfortable." They examine the critical connection between innovation and leadership.

Q: Apple is one of the few companies in the Fortune 500 to have a Senior Vice President of Design. Why?
Design is one of the essential tools Apple has. For most companies, design is possibly the function least understood and most difficult to manage successfully and consistently. Successful companies understand the importance of design in the success of their business. Apple, Virgin, Nissan and Lincoln are all in different business categories, but all share the concern for a healthy relationship with their customers. But how? How do you create new meaningful engagements that deliver a competitive advantage? Today, people speak about the Apple program as being "**obvious in retrospect.**"

Obvious in retrospect What comes to mind here is the concept of resonance or empathy in which the customer "feels felt". This is almost exclusively based on how each individual experiences the interaction. What Tim is pointing out is that by focusing on the total customer experience as being part of the human experience, the connection with the customer creates the experience of "feeling felt". The relationship moves from being "salesperson to customer" to a much more "person to person" dynamic.

It is as much to say it is as an enormously important design solution as it is the definition of great experience. To be "obvious in retrospect" means you have achieved a fit with the company and the people they wish to have a relationship with. It is a great way of thinking about whether the design or experience has had the greatest kind of impact and level of appropriateness as a solution. It is a good question to refer to consistently. Is your solution obvious in retrospect?

Companies must create a meaningful experience because we use design to better connect with their business targets. Design is the common thread. If you know how to use design to create positive human outcomes then you can use this to add value to your business. The best companies understand how valuable design can be and elevate the user experience to a high level in the decision-making process.

Q: How do the experience realms work together?
The four experience realms are interconnected and mutually supporting – the Services realm includes products, services and behavior, Place includes the architecture, interior design or physical touchpoints and Communications the digital or other forms of communications. Each of these areas needs to be considered in context with each other. Every successful relationship begins with the values that people share. In person-to-person relationships, the best bonds are between those who share universal values.

The experience is held together with the values of the brand, as the adhesive. Most businesses are not naturally structured this way. If they are, the intersection occurs mostly at the executive level. We have often found the need to translate the brand values into experience principles that are actionable; principles the company can apply to decision making and experience management. These principles serve to view the successful application of the brand values within the experience realms.

In typical branding development programs, we see very similar words rising to the top: simple, innovative, human, etc. These types of words are selected as they offer broad and valuable definitions of the brand but are extremely difficult for teams to implement. If I am a manager of a marketing or communications team of consultants there are many ways to interpret "innovation" for example because the term is so broad. These terms are typically the product of a group decision-making process so the words that can mean the most to the most people can also be the most difficult to turn into actionable reality. What is critical is that interpretation needs to connect with people. In many ways, the experience must embody those qualities for the company to connect in a meaningful and distinctive way.

Applying the term "experience" to business and consumers isn't new. In 1998 Joseph Pine and James Gilmore heralded the arrival of "the experience economy" in their controversial Harvard Business Review essay. They recognized that businesses that connect with their audience on a more holistic, emotional level will foster more memorable, meaningful, and rewarding relationships. This perspective accompanied the emergence of a new generation. The possibilities of emerging technologies have radically changed people's needs and expectations of the world around them. As a consumer, one is more informed, less loyal, and desires to dictate the terms on which they engage with businesses. A dialogue, not a monologue. Fluidity not friction. Experiences not objects.

> "Seventy-eight percent of millennials would rather pay for an experience than material goods." —Harris Poll

Q: The Lincoln China work was interesting in that you describe a similar condition in the automobile category as Lincoln having "last mover advantage." Can you explain?
Lincoln wanted a new automotive retail experience in China. It was looking for a new way to enter the Chinese market. Our process began with defining insights with the broader market, design studies, and testing to help Lincoln adequately positioned itself in the market prior to setting any physical design solutions. They asked us to look at how we could help make the Lincoln company a success in China. For us, it meant defining the Lincoln experience holistically.

They were one of the last existing luxury car brands to come to China, which was seen as a disadvantage, but we saw it as an advantage. Last-mover advantage. To do what all the other car brands had done, to follow the competitors, would have made them one of many. That would have put them at an incredible disadvantage in the market. For Lincoln this would be a key to entering a market where virtually all of the primary luxury car brands were already established. The good news was that all the competitors were selling cars the same way luxury cars have always been sold. But people today are buying products, including cars, in new ways. Most people in China today search information and create configurations on mobile devices. This was an opportunity for Lincoln to separate from the others. Something we have started to explore as an approach to other categories of retail in China and begun exporting to other programs around the world.

Our goal was to change the way people would think about buying cars with Lincoln—from transactions to relationships this was to transform the Lincoln experience to better express the values of the company and elevate the qualities that distinguish it from the other automobile brands. We looked for a new strategy to sell cars, ultimately, creating "The Lincoln Way." We had to use the existing Lincoln cars, the products, and build a distinct service experience that mattered to the new Chinese buyer.

We designed the environment—from the street to the presentation space in the service spaces—but with a completely new experience. We looked at several inputs, conducted interviews and workshops, and reviewed the research. The only thing scoring lower than a car buying experience in China was a banking experience. We recommended a new behavior model. Rick Baker, Lincoln China's General Manager at the time, supported us and led the project with his team. It was courageous, intelligent and ultimately was successful. It meant taking on **the established way** of doing things.

The established way. This is a very good example of how a dealership can embrace the primary risk based on its understanding the primary task. The primary task was to come up with an innovative approach, a completely new way of selling cars. An approach that would deeply resonate with the target customer base. The new behavior model that Tim referenced carried with it a considerable amount of risk; the risk of "getting it wrong". By redefining the customer experience and focusing on hospitality there was indeed the risk that it would not resonate with the customers. By identifying and addressing this risk, Lincoln was able to engage in the innovative design while also being conscious of possible unintended negative reactions. Being aware of this reality enabled them to keep the customer in mind rather than to blindly advance an innovative approach that would not resonate with the target market.

One of the first approaches we looked at in the behavior model was taking the salespeople out of the showroom. From a physical perspective we designed the space to reflect a more intimate scale than the competitors, in order to present the product with respect and in the best light. Make it warmer and personal to express the heritage and amazing legacy of the Lincoln Automobile Company. We also proposed a shift from a traditional dealership model to a hospitality model.

Q: You recommended to eliminate salespeople in the car dealerships?

Yes. This part of our proposal surprised Lincoln. As a way to shift the experience at Lincoln we proposed to eliminate sales people in their retail program. Maybe they aren't needed today. We looked very carefully at the target audiences Lincoln wanted to serve and tried to understand them. Sales were needed. Salespeople were not. We replaced salespeople with hosts—a fundamental shift from a transaction focus to customer focus on hospitality. This is something that companies in the hospitality category do incredibly well and that people associate with luxury.

Digital access to the information has enabled customers to know more about the details of the car, competitors, specifications, etc., than most of salespeople know. Car salespeople are consistently rated at the bottom of the list of preferred customer interaction ratings. Eliminating them meant we could fundamentally change the car buying experience. This enabled us to look at the guest journeys in a way to better connect with pre, during and post-purchase activities simultaneously in physical and digital spaces. This also left open the opportunity to redefine a new and distinct behavior model. How people interact with others in the company and what should the roles and responsibilities should be.

Fortunately for us, the competitor car manufacturers were selling cars the way they had been for years. The good news for Lincoln was people were buying cars differently. Most were configuring the models in advance of visiting a showroom on their mobile devices and had more current information than the car sales staff, often creating an awkward knowledge gap and ultimately not creating a positive brand experience. People needed support not pushing.

We saw an incredible disconnect in the typical car buying experience. People were going online to browse and configure vehicles before traveling to the outskirts of the city (where, by law in China, all service dealerships are located) to view, touch, and test drive. With the integration of one size fits one single user experience, a Mono-channel or Live-channel distributed retail ecosystem that bridges digital space and physical space, we had to respect the time people had spent configuring and interacting in the digital realm and elevate the connectedness in the physical area. We created digital tools in the Lincoln showrooms that recognized and could illustrate a previously configured vehicle, and transcend the physical limitations of the digital devices.

In one piece of research we found most people in the target segment would refer to a nationwide popular restaurant chain as delivering a great user experience. They consistently defined HaiDiLao, a "HotPot" restaurant as a luxury experience in China. We went there multiple times to experience what part of that experience contributed to a good luxury experience in China. Why was this experience perceived as luxurious?

For HaiDiLao, much of the details in the experience reflected unusual interactions with the guest. The staff are uncommonly connected to the customers. They engage them in personal ways unlike most service staff throughout the country. We observed that a primary engagement included personal touch when providing apparel to protect the diners clothing from the boiling hot pot, engaged the customers with simple things such as eye contact, warm conversation and smiles. These services are not very unique to human interactions, but as the embodiment of what a personal service experience is in China, they are.

The basis of the experience became the fundamentals we included in the behavior model we created to define the Lincoln Way. It required a new series of roles and engagement to activate and differentiate Lincoln from the other luxury brands in the category. In defining the Behavior Realm for a company is it essential to align the interactions and postures to express the brand values through the interaction. This pattern of behavior is critical to define the distinctive aspects that separate the company from its competitors in the same way as the experience at HaiDi-Lao does with its customers. Understanding cultural differences may be the key to success and failure.

Q: Is focusing on the customer experience just a frill?
When businesses anything beyond baseline as a frill, it's often the accountant's perspective. It's not much of a leadership perspective, however. There is no customer experience in the equation. Looking at the numbers gives us the ability to project possible outcomes, but without customer value, at the core, it is impossible to run a great company from that perspective.

As Joe Pine points out and research frequently supports, most people have moved to a purchasing experience over the product. From the functional objectives, which are now assumed to be a baseline requirement, to an aspirational and experiential engagement with the company. To not consider focusing on customer experience is only short-sighted and a missed opportunity in the competitive environment. As competition increases, the experience can be a crucial differentiator to change the perception of the value offered. From the business perspective, it's likely more important to focus on ROE (return on experience), to achieve better ROI (return on investment).

Q: How does a focus on customer experience create value?
Through distinction and emotional connections. Some people have defined Steve Jobs as a customer experience savant. I share that view. He understood how to create value and how to approach problems. Parity in any industry is not suitable for that business category. Parity is often part of the natural progression that is a compounded negative when sales or revenues decline. Experience drives consumer behavior and can distinguish the values and products of one business over another. Loyalty disruption occurs because of transparency and ubiquitous communications. Experience is one aspect that does not rely purely on logical justifications but resonates at an emotional level.

Customer experience alone is not the only tool for success. Without a meaningful product it is impossible to truly achieve the lift a great brand experience can give you regarding economic value. Loyalty and passion for a company will sustain through experiments in product and allow forgiveness for the inevitable misstep.

Apple Genius Bar, Tokyo, 2003

Irrational Loyalty

If we had followed the retail conventional wisdom, we would have never built the iconic 5th Avenue Apple store. It has no products in the windows, it's located in a basement, which was two blocks from the primary shopping streets.

REGENT
HOUSE

Apple Store, London, 2004

235

Apple Store Fifth Avenue, New York, 2006

Apple Store, New York, 2007

Apple Mini Store, Palo Alto, 2001

Apple Mini Store, Palo Alto, 2001

MacBook Air

Apple Store, Paris, 2012

Apple Store, San Francisco, 2013

Apple Store, London, 2013

Re: Store your min
body, spirit, energy
ideas, perspectives
mood, state, soul, t
love, life.

OUE Re:Store Branding, Singapore, 2016

OUE
Re:Store

Re: Chef Sau Del Rosario
Re: Chef William Wongso
Re: KF Seetoh
Re: Chef Sun Kim

Now this is what I call ...
Beef Rendang
Chef William Wongso

Re:

OUE Re:Store Branding, Singapore, 2016

Two Rooms Grill Bar, Tokyo, 2019

Two Rooms Grill Bar, Tokyo, 2019

COACH

Coach Ginza Flagship Store, Tokyo, 2004

MIZUHO

Gap Ginza, Tokyo, 2011

Gap Ginza, Tokyo, 2011

Q: Is good design about building advocacy?
All design has a point of view. If the view is meaningful, it can point to a kind of activism. Designers are often given a chance to have an impact on many people's lives. It's part of a role we choose to undertake as designers. It is our choice to set those goals of course but, in design, the purpose of creating new things comes with more than personal responsibility. That is because, in the best of cases, design can change things in a positive way, but we also must understand any unintended consequences. As a result, we need to determine how our solutions lead to more positive outcomes. It's crucial for the design to work with those people who are interested in those objectives. I believe you have to decide if what you are doing adds to a positive outcome. Sometimes it means setting ridiculously ambitious goals.

Q: Is that realistic? It's not impossible, but isn't it improbable to have impact in everything you do?
Be careful what you aim to achieve. Best case you achieve it. Without a meaningful goal, you should question why you are undertaking it. Designers approach problems when they receive a design brief that identifies a list of outcomes your clients hope to achieve: more transactions, more customers, more money. We need to reframe those business outcomes into human drivers that lead to the business objectives. Is it realistic? Clearly, but only if you choose to bring that into the problem you are looking to solve. For every situation, there is an opportunity to look at what positive impact the design can achieve. As an activist, you take on a vision of how the world should be, and look at how to build more meaningful design. Ideally it will activate others to perform in a way that brings others into that ideal.

Q: A few years ago, there was a survey of the top 10 highest paid CEOs in America. Out of those selected, six of the 10 were Eight Inc. clients. How is it that some of the most progressive leaders come to work with you?
We have grown globally due to the results that contributed to the growth and success created through strategic design. Eight Inc. has been fortunate to work with some amazing people including some of the leading CEOs and figures in the business world. In large part, we help them

create value. I think it has to do with a shared recognition of the relationship between people and value creation. If you do this successfully and consistently you attract people who appreciate the outcome and value.

Not only value in the financial sense, although that is an outcome, but value for people. We create a better way of doing things. These solutions create human value and that ultimately translates to the business.

Not only value in the financial sense. Again, we see a great example of the distinction and understanding of the primary task. Far too often leaders think the primary task is financial but indeed financial success is an outcome and not a goal. The goal is to be seen as adding or creating value. If people perceive what you are offering as adding value, they will be willing to engage with you and that engagement will result in financial success. But the primary task remains adding value. Conversely, the moment that a company is seen as not adding value or indeed even destroying value, customers will disengage and ultimately this disengagement will result in financial loss.

Q: What is the common thread for each of these types of CEOs.
I think it's true leadership versus management. It's a focus on what the business does that creates value. What the product does for the user. It transcends the management role of the CEO. The best leaders share similar qualities and the connection to the relationship between people, products and services, and must have a genuine value. They listen. They usually understand the best outcomes will be when the people they employ for their projects are allowed to work from their strengths. They understand human behavior at a deeper level than most others, and recognize the structural nature of a business to deliver the business objectives.

Simon Sinek talks about a deep understanding of human psychology and biology to describe how successful leaders are so valuable. His "golden circle" articulates the way we communicate and the way it links to how we feel and understand things—defining why we do things. Great leaders possess these skills either overtly or intuitively. Ernest Cu, CEO at Globe Telecom in the Philippines is a great example. Our first contact was a lengthy discussion about understanding each other as people first, before we jumped into the business challenge and working together. This is not the only CEO who has engaged us this way. It usually indicates the opportunity for a successful relationship and a successful design.

For Globe, the business grew from 23% market share to 56% in two years thanks to the new way of connecting the brilliant people at Globe with the people of the Philippines.

Q: Is it always important to work with the CEO or someone at the very top?
It makes a big difference. Most businesses are structured to operate in separate verticals, and it is at the C-level that most of the business aspects converge. There is usually not someone who is responsible for the customer experience explicitly. Some companies struggle to work outside of those verticals. At Apple, with Steve Jobs it worked because Steve was the decision maker and ultimately focused on how all the elements when they came together delivered an extraordinary experience. Again, the company was much smaller than it is today. But he was able to control that. When you think of other companies where it's a much more traditional corporate structure, you don't always get those kinds of immediate decisions. We can help reframe some of that responsibility.

Q: What are some of the specific changes you have seen to the client experience in the last 10-20 years, and what have these shifts meant for designers such as terms of approach, design thinking, etc.?
IBM research that pointed out the new world we live in: Uber, the world's largest taxi company, owns no vehicles. Facebook, the world's most popular media owner, creates no content. Alibaba, the most valuable retailer, has no inventory. And Airbnb, the world's largest accommodation provider, owns no real estate....

The rules of the game continue to shift today. There is far more complexity. Rate of change and technology are influencing new opportunities for new behaviors. Complexity and the ability for the little companies to take on the large ones is becoming less of an obstacle to compete. Focus on the customer experience is the only real differentiator in any market, new or old.

Obviously, there are those companies who are smaller and younger in the market that are looking at different ways to distinguish themselves from the competition. Some look to redefine a solution, think new world economy companies. Others explore areas—where others have given up are where they tend to see new opportunities. As new companies raise the bar on the user experience, the older companies either elevate their experience or will assume a predictable and inevitable decline, but likely decline in their company's value. Across the industry there are some that are consistently rated better than the others because of the human experience, the technology, and dependability, and a focus on service seems to be at the core of the way they operate. It's very much a function of what the company must provide to meet the expectations of their primary market.

Q: The design field seems to be experiencing disruption as well. What is your approach to this disruption?
I have seen at least two cycles of something like this in my career, where extraordinary design has created value for a business. This can be a challenge. Most businesses typically struggle with managing and orchestrating design, and respond by bringing creative teams into their organization. Apple revolutionized the business world with outcomes by delivering great user experience, and opened the world to democratized technology. Virgin to a new way to travel. Where there is success the response is predictably to imitate. Business brought in and built up large teams of designers to expand their growth and innovation, essentially following the perceived model of successful design-led companies. Most are unable to make the correct decisions and lead creative teams because leaders seldom come from a design sensitive or creative culture.

Q: Business models are being disrupted so how do you stay competitive?
We are at a time when there is a complete collapse of other formerly reliable business models. Most obvious in banking, traditional retail and advertising. With the design demand, advertising agencies gobbled up design firms and traditional consulting firms decided they could stem decreasing insight and distinctiveness by adding design thinking and purchasing design teams. Unfortunately, this makes for naturally odd conditions for success. Most of the truly creative leaders gradually migrate from the original agencies when the leaders of the businesses no longer truly appreciated the dynamics of creative individuals.

It's very difficult for many business leaders to lead design teams for example and vice-versa. Most of the strongest creative leaders exit the big companies to begin their own firms or join smaller higher quality boutique firms that have held a higher standard of quality and strategy. The cycle continues. The key is not *what*, but *how* to keep creative teams productive, valued and intact.

Q: How do you know if the design will lead to customers loving a company? Can you test for passion?
We conduct tests of concepts with people companies want to connect to, both early in design and the development stage, but also later. And then we try to ask ourselves how it is not just unique but meaningful. Not different for difference sake but is it improving or offering a unique advantage over the competitors or improving people's experience with the company?

You cannot always know if it will work. This is why you need to understand where the risk is and be able to learn from what others experience. When we did the Apple store in London, there were many who slept outside the night before it opened in the cold and wet weather. The fourth person in the line was actually a 73-year-old woman who lay in her sleeping bag alongside many other young people. We invited her in, to be more comfortable. She declined. She told me that she just had to be there. With the others who loved Apple at this moment. She wanted the experience something that could only happen once for her. She told me she loved the company. This is irrational loyalty.

Q: The design of the Apple Store on 5th Avenue in NY is iconic. Tourists frequently take pictures of themselves in front of it. Its sales per square foot are the highest in the industry: $4,551—more than any other store of its kind. It does this by breaking many of the established rules of the retail trade—just as Apple has always done.
If you look at the first design, it was the pinnacle of the program at that time. It helped give physicality to the company that is one of its most valuable touchpoints. The initial cube design was made of three vertical panels of glass. Part way through the development we were able to source single large sheets of glass but it was too late in the construction

schedule to implement. When Steve knew he may not survive his illness he knew this was one of his legacy projects and ordered a new cube made with the single sheets to replace the multiple panels. This is how dedicated he was to creating a perfect execution in anything he was involved in. The Apple 5th Avenue store became an expression of superior technology—advanced and distinctive. It set a bar in retail that few have ever met. Many people have formed opinions about **why Apple retail** was such a success.

Why Apple retail. The Apple store experience "works" because there is a deeper understanding of the customer's desire for feeling connected and being part of a community, which is exactly what occurs when one enters an Apple store. In fact, it doesn't feel like a store but more of a community experience.

We tend to believe the experience of being in an Apple place is fundamentally distinct, in communicating technical capability and accessibility for everyone. Ultimately these are the values the people who love the company believe in.

Q: While the experience is distinctive the design also violates many of the "conventional wisdom" rules of retail, but it still works. Why is that?

The space is in a basement. There are no products in the window and it is two-thirds of the block off what was the primary shopping street in New York City. The pundits of the program, before it launched warned Apple shareholders of the potential of losing millions of dollars on this retail "experiment". It was recommended that it would be smarter to give the money to the shareholders. This "wisdom" was a function of looking at the past versus the future. Because it had not been done previously it was deemed risky. The real **risk** of Apple retail would have been not creating the program.

Risk. The primary task and the primary risk are clearly seen in the decision to embark on the "retail experiment". Clearly there was a significant risk of "getting it wrong" and in fact many experts in the field predicted that it would be a failure. Yet Steve, while recognizing and identifying the risk of failure saw the greater risk of not continuing to evolve and of not engaging with the customers in a manner that redefined the retail experience. The primary task required that Apple embark on a different trajectory in order to "meet the customer where they are".

The real danger would have been to listen to the pundits, to not try. Without the retail program it is questionable if the company would be what it is today. At the time Steve accurately predicted that the cost of this store was not a factor. He was correct. The 5th avenue store was the landmark statement that Apple had arrived.

Q: What was the design process like?

The process was the same one we have employed for years. We went from very broad views of what the retail experience could be, to progressively more detailed design elements. As with most projects we would iterate many versions in drawings and models before settling on the physical mock-ups. Defining experience is something that must be looked at from a holistic experience perspective. The overall program development went through radical shifts at the beginning and we soon moved into the standards and versions of the standards that would be deployed globally. Many architects around the world would deploy the standards we created. Gensler, Bolin Cywinski Jackson and many others have been responsible for specific locations around the world as the program has grown. Now Foster and Partners are designing the new flagship retail spaces. The real difference here from other companies was the level of focus on detail and depth of the conversations. Today, Eight Inc. is consistently refining that process and delivering results across many different categories of business.

Q: You said that Steve was naturally nervous the night before the first store opened.
It was an amazing time. None of us were really sure what to expect the first day. We had just finished the first store, working late into night and setting up all the products and the lighting and adjusting everything. Steve was sitting on one of the tables and we were just gathering around him. He said, "Guys, **what happens** if nobody comes tomorrow?" And we all looked at each other thinking, "Can that be possible? Why ask now?"

What happens. This is clearly one of the best examples I've ever seen of how a leader needs to embrace the potential risk involved in innovation and creativity while also maintaining the course. The fact that Steve was able to express his concern and anxiety shows tremendous trust and courage as well as vulnerability. One could see the primary task as being connecting with the customer in a way that truly resonates and builds a relationship. The primary risk is as in all cases, the risk that "we got it wrong". What Steve was doing in this situation was openly acknowledging this possibility. By doing so, he was sharing his vulnerability as well as his humanity AND creating the space within that team to feel, reflect and think.

At the time Bloomberg published the opinion that the retail program was going to be a big disaster for Apple. It wasn't without a certain degree of risk and it was very visible. At that time Apple had only 2% market share. He may not have been 100% convinced that it would be as successful as it became. That's something that speaks to the kind of the character and the vision that he had. He would take that risk if he felt it was right. The analytics supported it but also the intuitive aspects supported it. Looking back on it today the real risk was not doing the program. The 5th Avenue Apple store in NYC did over $1 billion in sales last year. The real risk would have been to listen to the pundits and not do the program at all.

Q: Why do you think you were successful with him?
I think we have been successful there because there was trust. The most interesting thing about the work with any of our clients is getting to a point where there is a respect in the relationship and knowledge that they could rely on the work—a trusted partnership in a way. I believed we stretched the thinking when necessary and were not afraid to stand for what we believed in. Working with Steve was unique in many respects because of the way he thought about things. Because we began with him early when he returned to the company, we developed an under-

standing of his approach and his dual processing skill—both rational and emotional modes.

This strength was also a challenge to some who worked with him. When he would review work, I believed there were two modes that his thought process seemed to take. In many cases, his feedback centered around the rational or logical aspects of the idea. You could almost see him running through a logic tree to evaluate if the design had merit from a logical perspective. On the other hand he would just as easily approach the critique on an intuitive level—what did it make him feel. The greatest work possessed a resolved logic portion, as many designs that followed did, but the real magic was when the design made you feel something—that it mattered to you in a way beyond what you expected. If you were very competent at logic, you would be frustrated by an intuitive response to your work. On the other hand, if the creative work lacked thoughtfulness and rigor it would be seen and called out. Since most people are typically strong in one area it is difficult to work with someone who can look at a solution from both perspectives.

Q: In an interview with Marcus Fairs from *Dezeen* magazine you were famously critical that Apple retail development had slowed down. Can you talk about that?
It had an impact in the sense that many people were surprised. It was seen as being critical of Apple and the program we helped create. This was prior to Angela Ahrendts joining the team and the program was not evolving in those years. Most have misunderstood the point I was making in the interview. Many people (including some at Apple) thought I should not be critical of the leading electronics retailer or such a successful program we helped to create. Because this was for *Dezeen*, a design journal, I thought it was an important point to make.

Critical thought is an essential aspect of any successful design outcome. Criticism is healthy and always important in design. You have to have a certain degree of humility to create great things. You must be thoughtful about what you are creating and understand the context of the design. Steve Jobs was the most critical person at Apple on things Apple created and its industry. Critical thought was essential to his success. It led to great insights on customer experience and the way Apple would compete in the marketplace. Critical thinking is vital to great design, including Apple. When making anything better you have to question and re-question what you are doing. You need to ask why consistently. What is the value you are creating?

Q: How important is disruption in retail?
The best companies are **disrupting their own business** before the competition does.

Disrupting their own business. This again connects to adaptive leadership, the capacity to continuously be open to changing, adapting and questioning what has been established, while at the same time being respectful and protective of the organizational DNA that is fundamental and core to the organization or design. Too often we rationalize our fear of challenging our products or designs by convincing ourselves and others that it is fundamental or core to the DNA, and as a result we remain stuck in desperately trying to hold on to what is no longer value adding. The fear of "letting go" can be very strong and results in a resistance to change. Hal Gregersen's recent book *Questions are the Answer*, emphasizes the importance of questions in terms of driving disruptive innovation and change. By engaging in a "Question Burst" we increase our chances to identify a "catalytic questions" which will, by its very nature, result in significant and disruptive change.

From that *Dezeen* interview I mentioned that the Apple retail program was not evolving as fast as I felt it should be, I indicated that, "Since Steve [Jobs] passed away the momentum has slowed down a bit." This is natural. It was also imperative for Apple to continue to press forward again because the competition was pushing hard to catch up.

Retail business is always incredibly competitive, and most of the competitors have made a run to compete at company-owned retail channels. When you look at retail, you typically have to reinvent and disrupt yourself or you risk someone else doing it. Generally, companies usually look to refresh [retail touchpoints] every five years. If you're not reinventing it, you're losing your advantage. Steve was always very driven to stay an arms-length ahead of everyone else, so that once you got ahead you stayed ahead. And I think many of the competitors have made rapid changes to either emulate aspects of the Apple store or to be in the market in a much more significant way.

Another key point really was the failure of the competitors to step up. Apple retail had been very fortunate that it set the bar very high. Those other competitors had not been able to surpass what was such a successful retail experience. Many of the competitors in the consumer electronics category had looked to copy or emulate Apple rather than invent a new, more meaningful experience of their own. This is always the easy way but seldom the best way. They learned it is nearly impossible to out Apple, Apple. Each competitor learned another valuable lesson. The best way to keep the leader ahead is to become a follower. Fortunately for Apple, most of their direct competitors followed them rather than define their unique brand experience.

Nissan Crossing, Tokyo, 2016

Complexity

Design is contextual.

"In the military they give medals to people who are willing to sacrifice themselves so that others may gain. In business we give bonuses to people who sacrifice others so that we may gain. We have it backwards."
—Simon Sinek

Nissan Crossing, Tokyo, 2016

Nissan Crossing, Tokyo, 2016

Nissan Crossing, Tokyo, 2016

Nissan Crossing, Tokyo, 2016

SingEx, Singapore, 2016

JR Vending Machine, Tokyo, 2010

JR Vending Machine, Tokyo, 2010

WELTMEISTE
威马汽车

Weltmeister Maker Lab, China, 2018

威马 EX5

Weltmeister Makerclub, China, 2018

Weltmeister Maker Lab, China, 2018

Weltmeister Maker Lab, China, 2018

Jumeirah
HOTELS & RESORTS
RESTAURANTS
Destination
Dates

Jumeirah Website, 2019

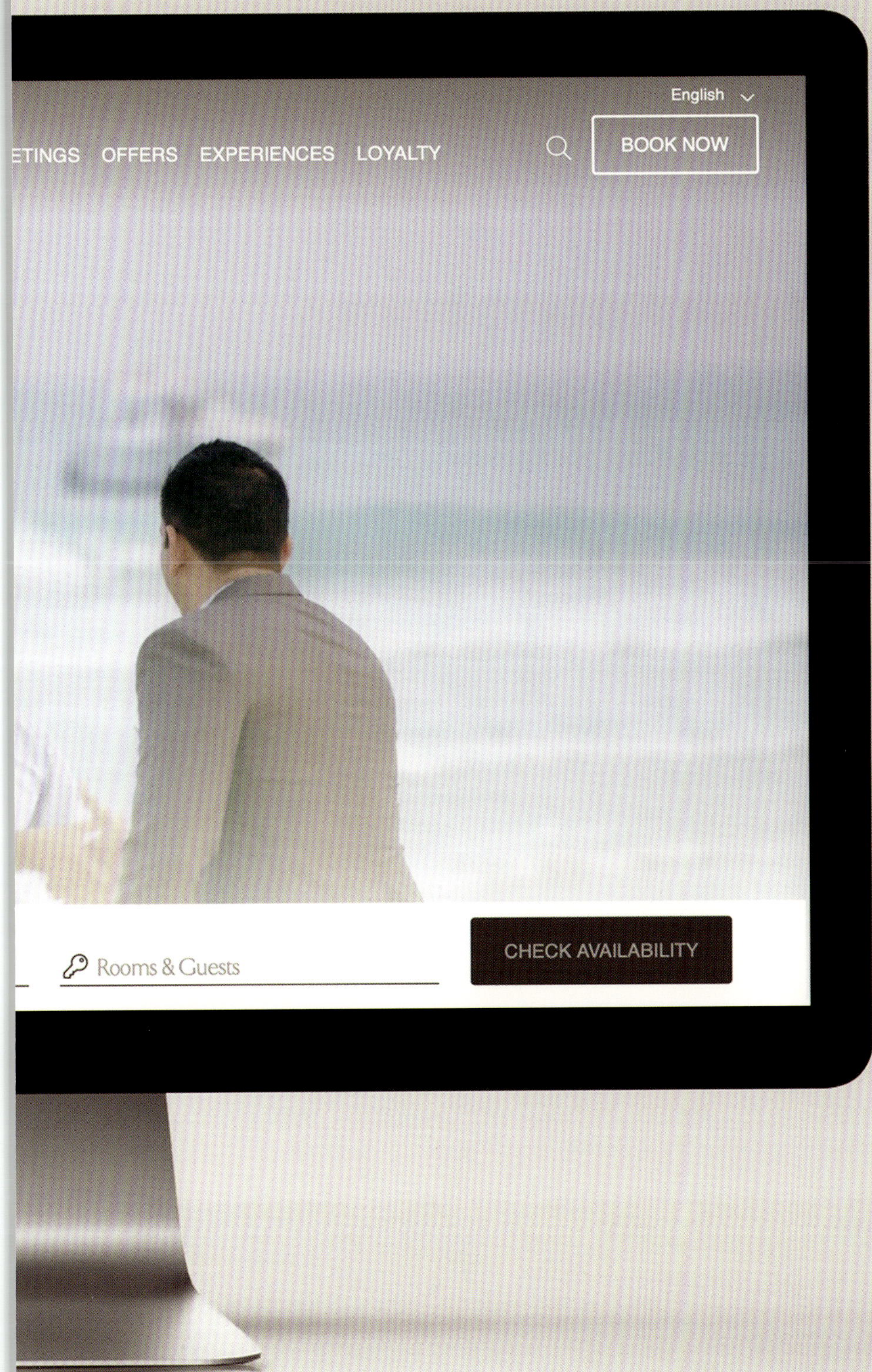

Jumeirah Website, 2019

Jumeirah Website, 2019

Style
Multimedia
Fã de música?

Nokia Flagship Store, Sao Paulo, 2008

Nokia Flagship Store, Sao Paulo, 2008

Nokia Flagship Store, Sao Paulo, 2008

Nokia Consumer Electronic Show, Las Vegas, 2008

Q: Things today seem to be more and more complex, with many moving parts. Are consumers and companies overwhelmed by most complex problems?
The perception of many different disruptive forces affecting a condition usually renders the user or viewer unable to process what the real problems are, much less understand the implications. This "noise" needs to first be clarified to understand the complexity of a before a successful design solution can be created. In design, we normally encounter multiple and often opposing factors that seem like overwhelming complex conditions. These influence the design, leading to a better way to view the influences and organize the insights. To not only understand but "feel" where the best outcome can be.

Q: Change is happening so rapidly that it seems impossible to keep up, much less lead.
In many cases, the problem may be exacerbated by the **rate of change.**

Rate of change. We are in a time where digital space is rapidly transforming design but technology in many areas is impacting our lives beyond what we could have imagined a few years ago. Digital and physical space have converged. We struggle because we tend to learn and understand things in silos. Products like the Apple Watch or Tesla are examples of intersections where we struggle with the implications and boundaries.

This change is often felt as forced upon by other outside forces and not typically welcomed. There is an opportunity here that can allows companies to be more appealing than their competitors by understanding the physiological state of their market and providing **relief** from this. Apple did this when the PC was overwhelming everyone but computer engineers.

Relief. In fact, people respond with tremendous resistance when they experience change as being forced on them. The clever companies are able to position the change as an "invitation" to join them in the "new". They offer a choice but are clear about the advantages of the change and its benefit for their customers.

Q: How do companies lead in this kind of environment?
The most successful companies have a team in their business looking at disrupting itself before the competitors do. They also have feedback systems in both the number of receptors or touchpoints to provide

insights to the business. It allows them to remain competitive and work out of a proactive rather than reactive posture. Sometimes this falls into R&D versus other operational verticals in a company. Often it is woven into the investment arm of an entity to identify new companies or technologies that will contribute to the changing landscape.

Q: How does design work with the complexity of transforming technologies and rapidly changing user expectations?
We are in a time when digital space is rapidly transforming design, but technology in many areas is impacting our lives beyond what we could imagine a few years ago. Digital and physical spaces have converged. We are just struggling because we tend to learn and understand things in silos. Products like the Apple Watch or Tesla are examples of intersections where we struggle with the implications

Q: You published a piece for Bloomberg on the future of mobility called "*A Case for the Third Dimension.*" You talked about what is after autonomous cars. Autonomous flight vehicles. What was that about?
It's about defining a sustainable future. We have a business unit called X8 Ventures that works on complex new ventures. It consists of both internal and external partnerships. One of our X8 Venture companies is looking at next generation mobility. Beyond electric cars, autonomous mobility. Everyone is focused on the mobility opportunity that technology can help mediate. It's progress, but solving for terrestrial mobility is incremental. Autonomous cars address efficiency but that is only part of the problem. Autonomous cars look to improve space utilization in a horizontal dimension, change our lifestyles and solve the challenge of 1.24m deaths globally per year in automobile accidents. An admirable ambition, but it does not address the fundamental problem—density. Mobility in densely populated urban environments grows globally and has an increasingly negative impact on our lives. The IEA projects 1.7 billion cars worldwide by 2035. Where do we put them? We have reached the limits of our two-dimensional space.

Soon it will be hard to remember a day when the two- dimensional world bound us in mobility. This case sees a short distance, point-to-point, versatile transportation designed to drive better human outcomes through better human experience. Traditional air travel has given us safe and consistent ways to move from different cities and countries. We will shortly see low altitude, multi-tier airspaces over our primary circulation arteries. Designed to support individual mobility needs, light load cargo, and transform our emergency care and service providers. Autonomous Flight Vehicles (AFVs) will shatter category norms through smarter interconnected systems. As with virtually every major category in our lives today, disruption is transforming in ways that we often struggle to comprehend. An AFV network part of a mobility ecosystem however will be part of a comprehensive mobility solution. Autonomous Flight Vehicles will be a disruption in a category that effectively defined incremental change.

For the first time in human history, we have a convergence of technology to make this opportunity a reality; electric, autonomous, connected, proven sensor-based flight technology, navigation controls in every pocket to utilize multi-verse navigation and control systems. Leveraging our distributed and secure wireless communications with a clear energy bias. Renewable energy systems designed to leverage existing distribution networks and deployable in a range of urban applications. It will be essential we take this opportunity to make life better. The inherent chance in this transformation is to solve for a better human experience. AFV's will find a fit into interconnected transportations systems working with the existing infrastructure investment and expanding our mobility performance with a dramatically reduced infrastructure investment.

With the future of mobility moving to the third dimension it will be hard to remember the limitations of the two-dimensional surface and what a true shift it was. The terrestrial plane will be transformed into space that supports quality of life, just as we have with residential or office applications—the built space. The areas we have dedicated previously to dense, slow-moving corridors of nearly motionless automobiles will transform into spaces that will support more cycling, interconnected green spaces, and spaces to connect our cities effectively but with better human outcomes. When the Wright brothers demonstrated man-powered flight, 14 seconds changed the world. For 2,000 years we had been trying to fly. Sixty-six years after the Wright brothers, we reached the moon. It's time for our mobility solutions to move from incremental change to a shift that accepts a more significant challenge, a better way to live.

Q: We are in an era of transformation in mobility solutions. Eight Inc. designed the Nissan Crossing project created an experience center to highlight the technology and future mobility solutions Nissan is developing.
Our recent Nissan Crossing project in Ginza, Tokyo is an excellent example of the human experience leading to business outcomes. It is an extensive experience center. Nissan wanted to transform their former showroom into an innovation center to be able to talk about their new technologies, autonomous vehicles, and green technologies, and they wanted to do it in a way that they could improve the number of people who would visit their sites. We proposed a subtle but significant shift in the experience. Most were content showing the cars that anyone could see at typical dealerships. For this we chose to feature mobility solutions of the future. The concepts and the explorations.

In the previous space, they would have 3,000 visitors a month come to this location. Nissan asked us to increase it by 33% to accommodate 4,000 visitors. We designed the space and developed new ways of presenting the vehicles in differentiated ways. Things that would drive some attraction into the space and start to connect people with what Nissan was about as company—and it is about more than just cars. There are opportunities both concerning physical and digital interactions as components within the experience, and they were a little surprised as we went from 3,000 to 250,000 visitors per month. Creating an experience that is compelling and attractive can have this exponential value in many cases.

Open since 2017, Nissan Crossing is now among the Iconic architectural destinations in Ginza. The design delivers an immersive experience unlike any other, and with the architecture of Klein Dytham the experience is focused on the Nissan tagline "Innovation that excites." The design focuses on the primary ways to translate the Nissan creative legacy into stimulation and sensation. Where visitors feel the strongest and most meaningful emotions that Nissan can deliver.

The challenge is to define a new level of engagement to see and feel Nissan, to be transformational and emotional with features that capture the exhilaration of the newest ideas and products that Nissan brings to the world. The arrival is a continuous revolving deck animating the entire corner of the Ginza Crossing. Meant to provide the visitor with exhilaration and participation around the continuously moving centerpiece of Ginza. It is part theater, part function, mostly fun, and a ride and anticipation for the next new thing. Bringing the magic of Nissan into a visceral and dynamic form and featured for all of those in Tokyo to enjoy. The experience was shaped around a number of distinctive and proprietary experiences to define the Nissan Crossing destination.

Q: Artificial intelligence is disrupting mobility in ways we did or could not imagine a few years ago. What do you think about the other possibilities of this technology?
Andrew Ng at Stanford says, "Artificial Intelligence is the next electricity." He implies AI will enable a great number of applications, but, as with any technology, what those applications become is a fundamental question. And the outcomes typically focused on human outcomes that benefit the most people usually offer the greatest value.

Q: We have seen the mega trends of mobile, cloud, social, and data come to fruition over the last 10 years and yet the pace of change seems to keep increasing. We are now in an era of internet of things, artificial intelligence, robotics, and so on. What are your thoughts on concerns around artificial intelligence?
Much of AI today is a capability looking for a purpose. Like any technology, its value lives in how well we design the application of it. Most forms are a technology looking for an application. The idea that the future of AI is somehow a polar opposite of human intelligence probably sells books, blogs, and podcasts, but it confuses the situation. I see artificial intelligence as a tool to enable greater human outcomes. But still far inferior to what the human mind can achieve.

Q: How can artificial intelligence create value?
Many companies, often infatuated with function over human outcomes, mistake technology for value creation. We live in a very competitive world. There are very few unique and successful ideas that do not get replicated very quickly. Designing human experience becomes immensely more valuable in an AI-enabled world. It's a differentiator. It's a way to connect with people in memorable and emotional ways.

Steve Jobs said, "The world's a very noisy place." It's hard for companies to separate from others—to drive distinction and relevance. I believe the opportunity for value creation with artificial intelligence will drive human outcomes through experience. It is fundamental to what artificial intelligence becomes. When I think of the value of human creativity, the ability to feel rather than think is essential. To infer, sense, to read between the lines, to challenge assumptions, and question authority, these are the qualities that help make us human.

Q: You are a persistent advocate of creativity. Is artificial intelligence capable of replacing creativity?
Creativity is one of the most valuable capabilities human beings possess. The reason for this is that it's essential for human progress. The tools it takes to create a creative solution is typically not something that lives in machine language. The works of great poets, painters, designers, dancers, or musicians were products of complex human experience, emotion, and insight. Experience, memory and disassociated connections. A machine can play all the keys on the piano but never replace the emotion that someone like Keith Jarrett plays with. More importantly it is challenged to create things without precedent. You can reprint the Mona Lisa but not create the next piece of artwork to move the human race forward.

The problem is originality. Most machine language is referential. It has precedent in some form to derive outcomes. I believe half of the potential of everything is the future. There is so much to be imagined that I feel there is a real challenge to using historical data and probability to generate "new" things. It's a form of reverse engineering. It's ironic that the most powerful and distinctive human **trait** is not linear.

Trait. Tim's reference to the most powerful and distinctive human trait not being linear brings into focus the fact that associative thinking is the birthplace of creativity. Causal thinking is basically looking historically and asking "why," which involves the linear system. Associative thinking however asks the question "what comes to mind" or invites the individual to not focus on solving a problem but allowing her or his mind, emotions, fantasies to emerge and become open to whatever might come to mind. In doing this we tap into the often unaccessed, unconscious part of our human capacity which links very much with creativity. Creativity is born out of associative processes rather than linear thinking.

While we currently don't have the capability to program "what has never been", we do have the capacity to create the space for the "what has never been" to emerge by means of associative thinking. This is why we believe associative thinking is the birthplace of creativity because it frees up the constraints that linear thinking imposes and allows our censored thoughts, ideas, possibilities and perspectives to emerge. Gregersen presents in his book *Questions are the Answer* is another avenue for surfacing new perspectives and ideas. Creative solutions often result from focusing on the questions and not the answers.

Consequently what emerges is a new way of doing, a new way of being, or a new way of engaging with the customer or the product. But it's messy, it's not something you can "make happen." At times it makes no sense, seems weird or completely out of touch with reality and yet it is those moments, those experiences that open us to the creative process that associative thinking brings forth.

There is a fundamental problem with using a linear system to create non-linear outcomes. How can you program for what has never been? People are always looking for a formula to replicate the creative outcomes by assuming a repeatable process. The day a machine can connect your unique personal memories and experiences, individual insights, skill, and intuition is the day there is a chance to make machines as rich as our humanity. A robot may be able to replace the hand but not the touch.

Q: Is artificial intelligence a threat to humanity?
Like other technologies, it can be both a threat and an opportunity. Realistically, AI today is immature and unreliable. Most algorithms are being used to determine whether not you get your housing loan, credit card, immensely, and not particularly nuanced at that.

Eric Schmidt talks about one of the areas of high value in the application of artificial intelligence being voice recognition. I happen to believe in a voice plus gesture applications but I am sure I have a bias towards more humanistic or natural interactions. Others talk about analytics' exponential value through quantum computing. The application of any of these technologies makes sense when you can enable a better outcome for people. Some are talking about the notion of artificial intelligence enhancing how and what we think about through greater insight—a sort of personal savant for each of us. Imagine the transformation of a social order built around ubiquitous access to not just information but relevant education. These are the kinds of applications that are interesting and exciting to me when I think about the possibilities of artificial intelligence.

The constant polar debate and the fear of the rise of the machine is a distraction. What we need to fear is how other people may be using this technology for their personal benefit at the expense of society. What people seem to fear is a lack of trust or control. The inability to control factors in your life that are critical to your individual opportunities and success. We are really just exposed to enough information to open the conversation.

Machines, and the way we think about artificial intelligence, are primarily based around the analytical processes of the brain. It's easiest to replicate, and it's the most linear. What's interesting to me is that space is only a small portion of what human intelligence can deliver. When I hear the discussion around machines taking away jobs and transforming our economies, this is really at a primitive level, and only the applicable to linear processing and most easily applied to more banal activities.

Remember the HP calculator was an early form of artificial intelligence. While we've come a long way in a short time, today we apparently haven't come far enough to understand human intelligence in order to establish the best of what artificial intelligence can achieve.

Artificial intelligence is a tool to enable greater human outcomes, but still far inferior to what the human mind can achieve. The human mind is not understood well enough to appreciate the kinds of flexibility and nuance it is capable of.

Citibank, London, 2011

An Idea Alone Is Not Innovation

I was asked about the value of the humanities. I think it's the value of the things that make us something greater than machines.

Dashboard Radar
Db
Dashboard
China Product X
Jane Smith
Sign out
Publications
Notifications
Inbox
New article
Brief overview of what Publications is lorom ipsum dolor sit amet.
Connect
New Message
Missed Calls
Alerts
Brief overview of what Connect is lorom ipsum dolor sit amet.

Citi Private Bank InView, New York, 2014

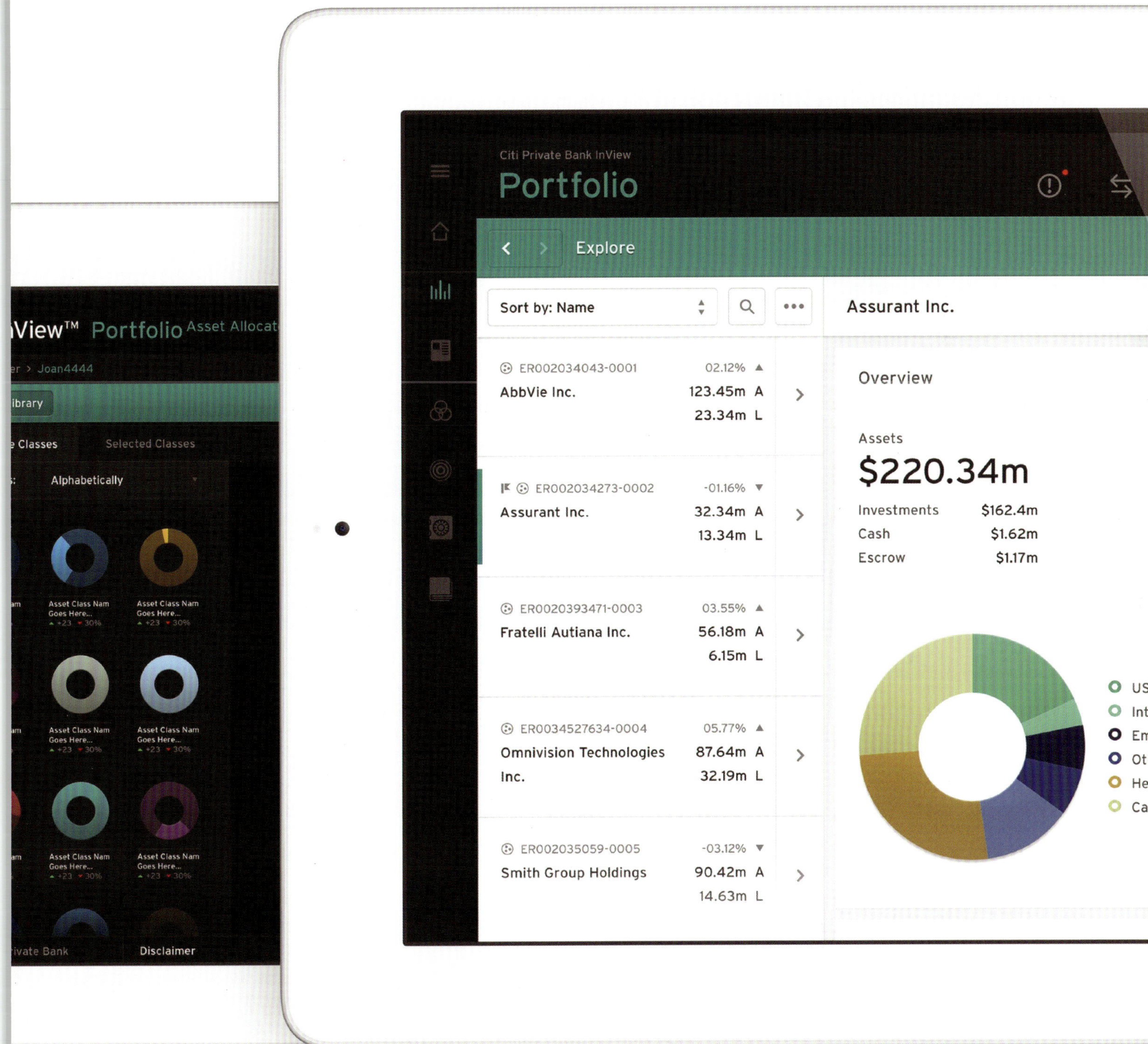

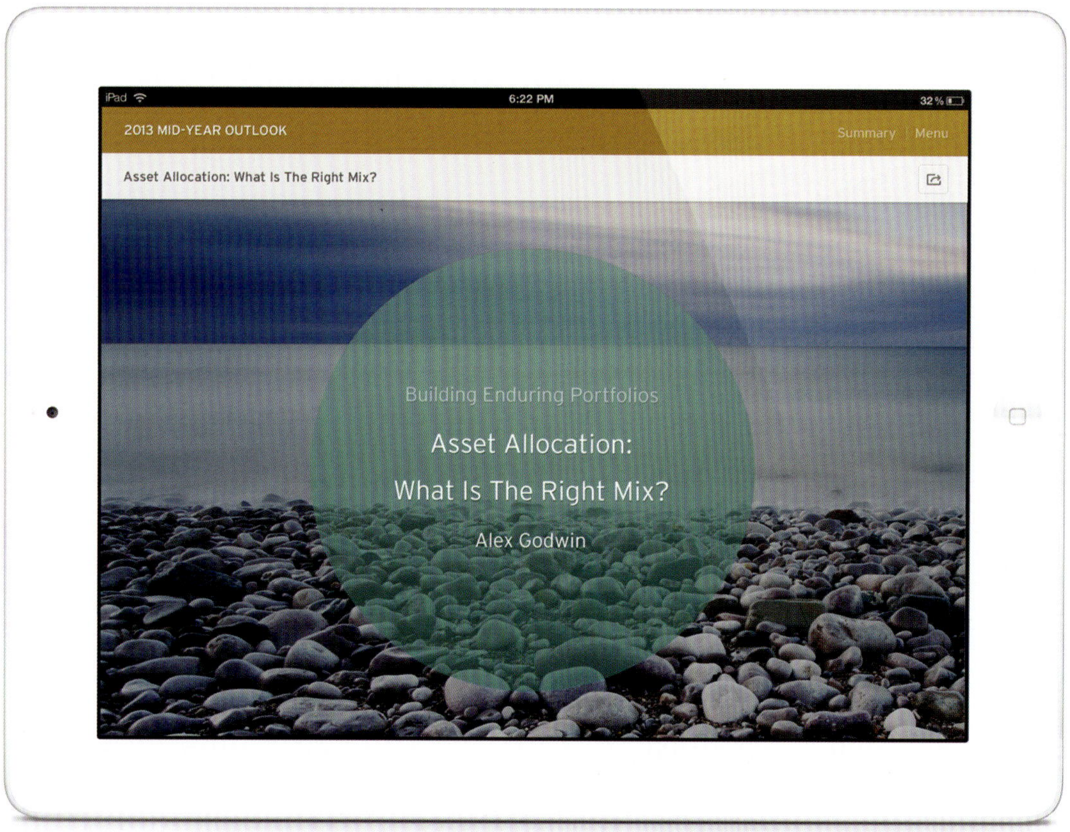

Citi Private Bank InView, New York, 2014

Citi Private Bank InView, New York, 2014

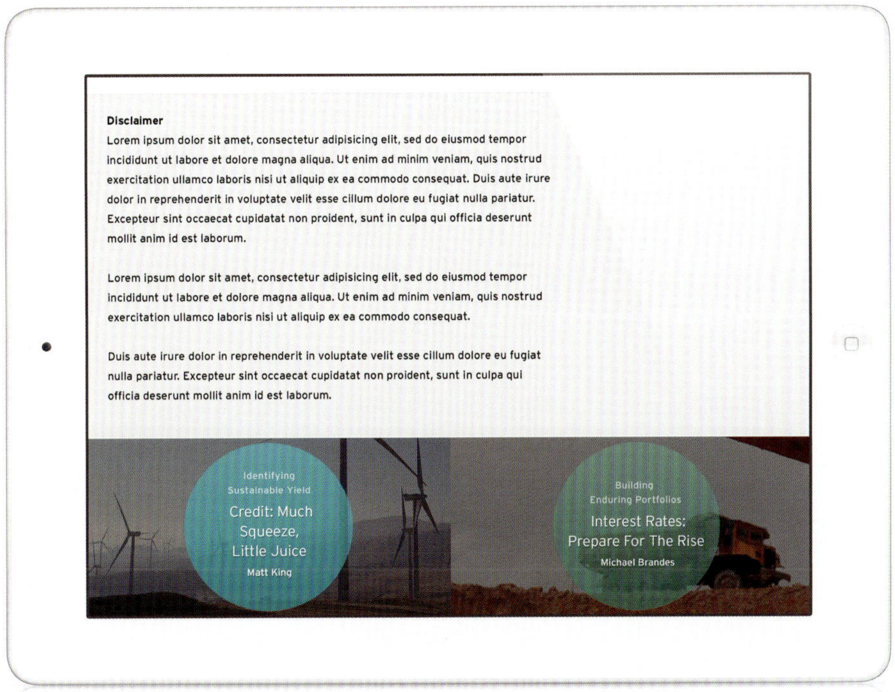

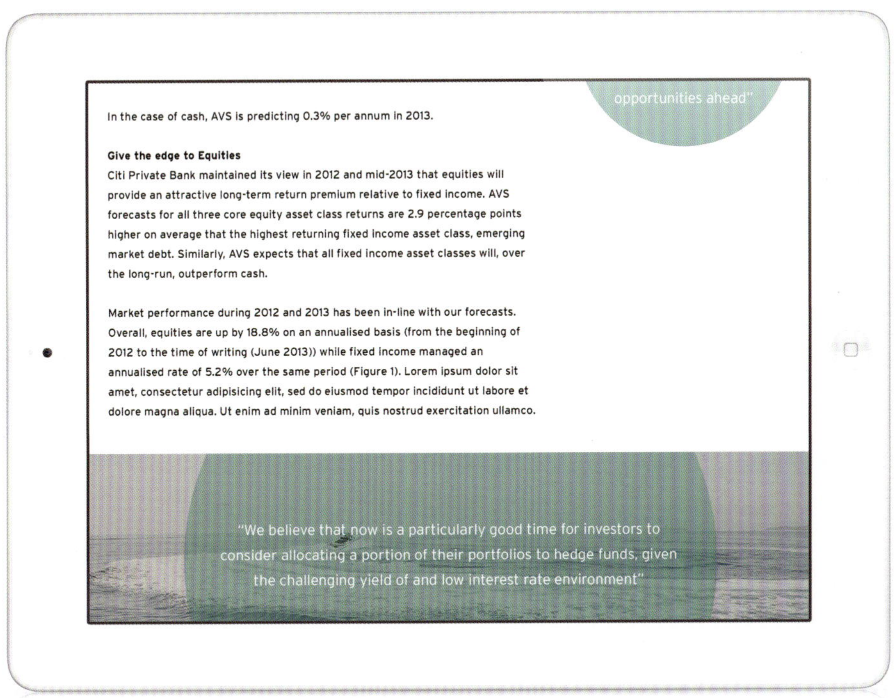

Airtel Next-Gen Retail Program, India, 2017

Can I get
a plan with
unlimited calls?

Devices
I want the best internet connection for my home or on the go (coming soon)

Airtel Next-Gen Retail Program, India, 2017

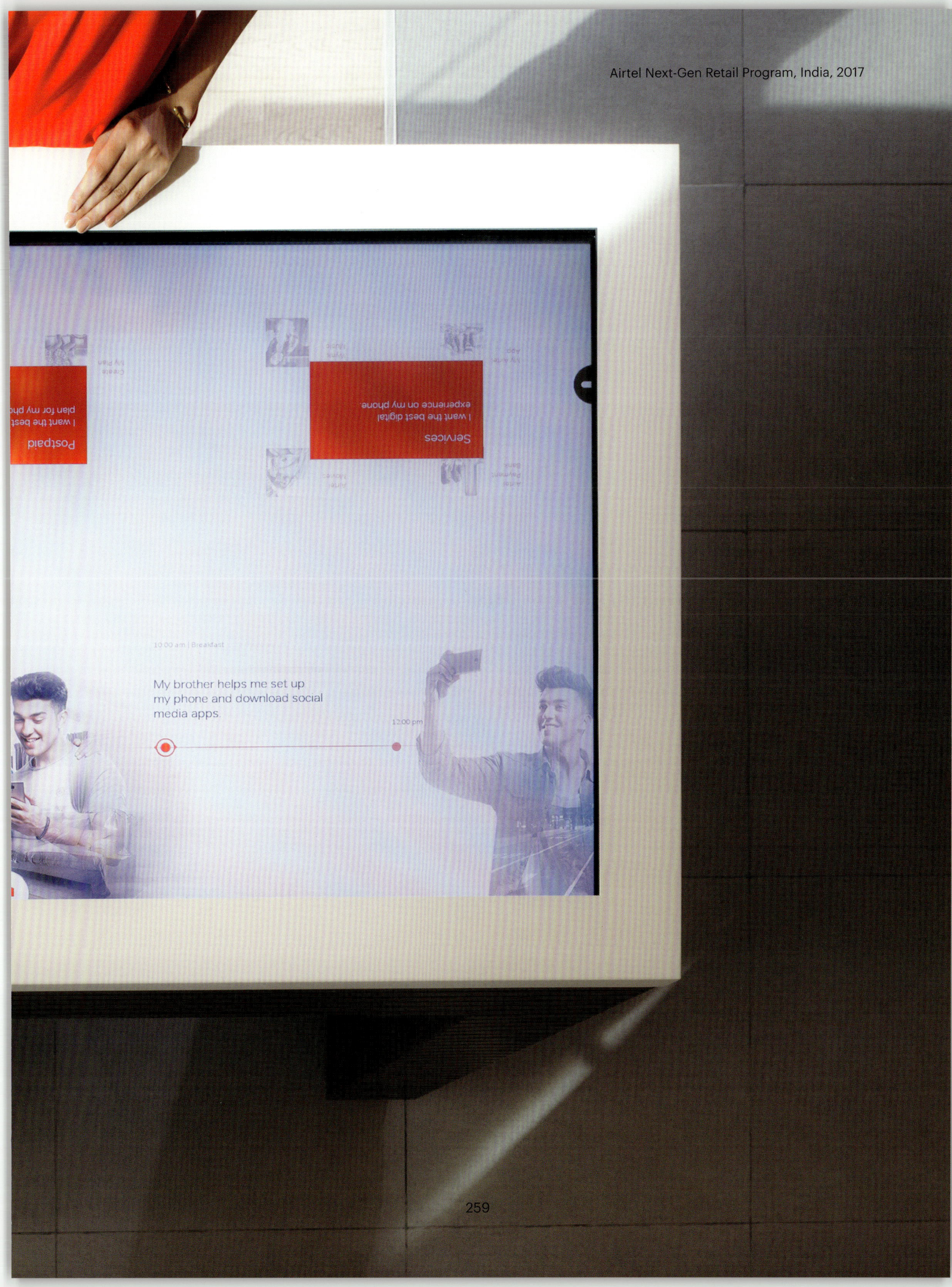

Chaayos
Wynk Music
Explore the network
Airtel Movies

Airtel Next-Gen Retail Program, India, 2017

S20 Bank, Seoul, 2012

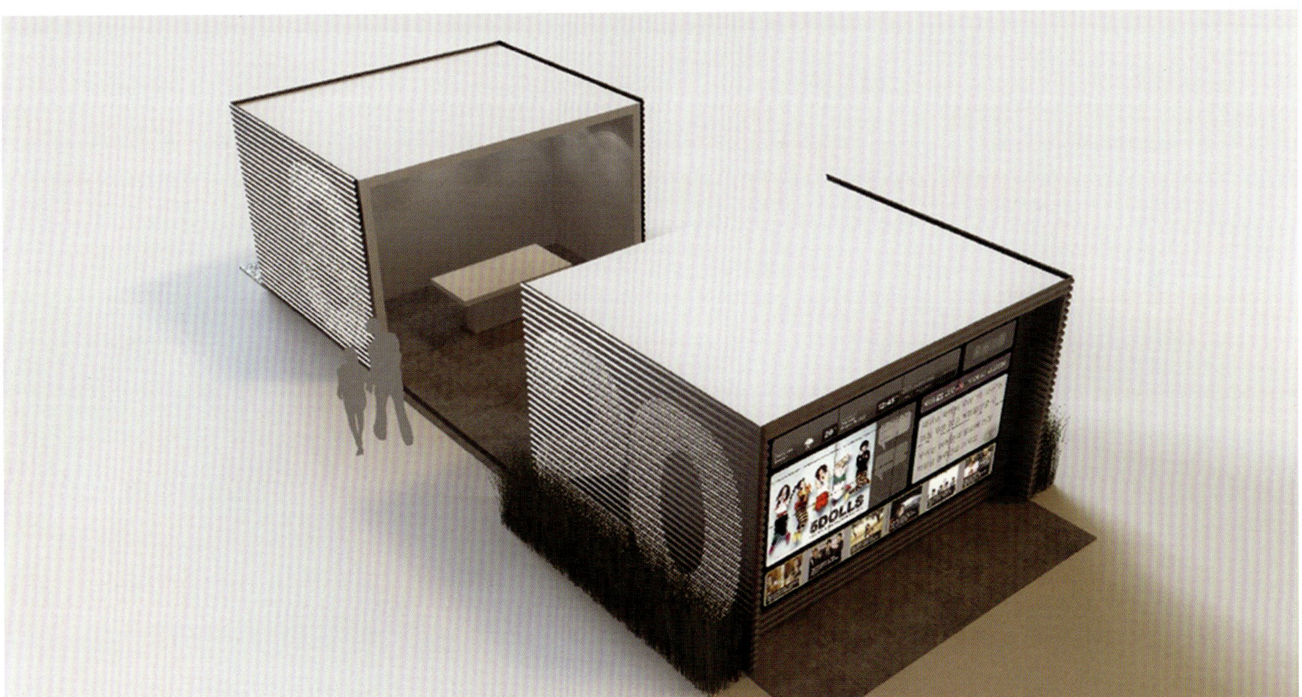

S20 Bank, Seoul, 2012

AKBANK
Gişe Ekstra
Artık Gişe Ekstra var, beklemek yok
Gişe
Ekstra
Gişe
Ekstra

Akbank, Istanbul, 2018

Akbank, Istanbul, 2018

Akbank, Istanbul, 2018

Citibank, Tokyo, 2009

Citibank, New York, 2010

Citibank, New York, 2010

Citibank, Tokyo, 2010

Q: Design thinking has become part of the business language today? Is it the same as design?
Design thinking as a term has been useful. It has helped bring design into more mainstream discussion. It's become a commonly misunderstood aspect of design however, because it's only a part of a design methodology. The more businesses are aware of the power of design to transform their business the better. We have seen many firms, companies, and governments employ design thinking as part of their process to identify and develop more meaningful solutions. As a part of a methodology it has merit but it is a starting point to identify important factors that will influence a creative solution. It's often seen as a solution in itself. A tactical "check the box" and it will be a success. Every linear thinker would love to have this type of way to understand the messiness of the creative process. We have often seen the disappointment in those who understood design thinking and thought it would solve their design problems and be the end of the design process. It simply will not.

There is a big difference between design thinking and design. The process of creation and innovation involves delivering a solution that leads to adoption or engagement. Without that it has little merit as being innovative. If you create things that people adopt because it changes their lives in a meaningful way, you add value. Adoption is the difference between Facebook and other social media platforms; between 160 different types of Nokia phones and one iPhone. A design has incredible power but needs to be considered with respect to great outcomes. Things that matter in some form, whether large or small.

Q: You say an idea alone is not innovation. Can you expand on that?
Innovation is contextual. Who knew we needed an Apple Genius Bar? Or Nespresso? We thought we already knew everything about coffee. Swarovski? Who knew we cared about crystals? An idea alone is just an idea. An idea is just the beginning. Execution of the idea that leads to success is innovation. Today's ideas, often the outcome of design thinking, are being mistaken for design. In some places, the design thinking proposition is having a negative impact on how people understand design. Their expectations of what a "post-it" thinking exercise should deliver are unrealistic. They are mistaking design thinking for design.

It's not the same thing. It is the start of any design challenge, but there is more to be done—the actual design. Design thinking delivers a process framework but it is not necessarily a successful business or human outcome. There is a gap there. Ideas are just part of the beginning of a design process. Without context, ideas do not really matter. Without skill and experience, an idea is simply a starting point. Design thinking is an excellent start but far away from innovation. Everyone has ideas, and that's good. But idea generation is simply a part of the beginning of a design process. You would never create a great meal by gathering all the best ingredients, inviting the perfect guests but not preparing, cooking, and sharing the meal.

When you think of delivering meaningful design, it takes more than framing the objectives and imagining new possibilities. It's a good start, and the initial observations and thoughts are often contained in an innovative solution, but seldom without significant impact on transformation based on the context and the delivery of the final thing. Designed outcomes are required for the application of a creative act: the work of exploring, testing, and failing; the consideration of the context, people, or activities in new ways; and the breaking of norms to arrive at new ones. Innovation occurs when people adopt a solution or behavior that changes the way they do things.

Great business leaders understand the difference in delivering meaningful solutions for people. It is a common thread among some of the great leaders we have known. Innovation is something that takes root in the fabric of people's lives. Adoption is the most significant way to define if something is innovative. Without adoption you cannot have meaningful human innovation.

Q: Can you describe your term anti-discipline?
When you think of the way we have traditionally defined our education and professional endeavors into verticals such as architects, industrial designers, communications designers, etc., it is a reflection of the thinking from the first industrial revolution. These disciplines are a product more of education or operational process than an outcome process. We are not anti-discipline but more interested in creating a nodal net-

work of T-shaped learners with expertise across disciplines, vertically and laterally. One of our clients described our work as creating things people love, and of course "love is undisciplined."

As design value is increasing, the design process has changed to reflect the nature of an increasing focus on human outcomes versus a focus on a purely consumption society. Bruce Nussbaum describes "aura" as a vital component of experience. In fact, it is the combination of elements a customer experiences in a way that builds passion and love. This is usually the softer parts of the creative process that makes many "business" leaders uncomfortable.

Q: When you think of innovative new products are there ones that come to mind? Which ones stand out in your mind?
Of course, the Apple iPhone changed the world. I can't think of a more impactful new product in recent times. When you see all the companies who have emulated the design, and scaled the extension of a mobile computing / communication and camera device into everyone's hand, it's hard to say there has been a more impactful product in recent times.

The iPod and iTunes revolutionized music and introduced the world to lifestyle platforms. We don't see transformational new products very often. It takes the recognition of unique conditions in technology and human experience. Technological advancements alone are not enough. Experience with the technology makes the difference. Other product innovations with incredible impact,—companies like AirBnb, Uber and Spotify—are companies who leveraged assets they didn't possess but understood the idea of underutilized resources.

Q: Let me focus the customer experience question on banking. Do banks really understand the power of customer experience?
I would say there is a difference between understanding the value versus delivery of good customer experience. Very few deliver it. When you say banks, you are talking about banks as an organization as opposed to individuals within an organization. Most banks today benefit when you fail. This cannot easily lead to a culture of human empathy. The idea that they are very much focused on themselves, their business, disrupts

the natural connection to providing those services for people. Recently banks have struggled to figure out where they should best operate. Beyond transactions, which are now commoditized, the question becomes about creating real value. I think this industry is one of the most challenged in delivering great customer experience.

Q: So, if they are struggling with customer experience, how can they improve it?
Align their success with their customers' financial success. The model will need to change. People talk about personalization, and that is one thing. Fundamentally, banks exist around a framework that has existed for a very long time with very little evolution. They are typically not technology leaders. In 2009 I said the bank of the future would be a technology company. In tech companies, I see a culture of striving for relevance and focus on customer experience there more than in traditional banking institutions. There are a many areas for improvement, hence the saturation of fintech offers.

Q: You mentioned personalization. How can banks deliver a personalized experience to the customer? I have read in a lot of articles saying that banks struggle with personalization. In your work with banks like ANZ, Akbank, Bangkok Bank and Citibank, etc. is there anything you've learned about how the banks can do this?
There are many ways of doing this. Putting customer first is a difficult one for most banks to reconcile. The first and greatest challenge is shifting the bank to become truly focused on **customer experience.**

Customer experience. The concept of "relationship" versus "relatedness" is extremely useful here. Historically, banks have not genuinely focused on the relationship with their customer but on the delivery of products. The result has been that the customers feel disconnected from the bank and have very minimal emotional connection; the bank becomes a "necessary tool" but there is minimal emotional resonance. There are not many people who feel passionate about their banking experience. It's a commodity and historically few of us feel "felt", understood and special. A friend recently shared with me "When I meet with my banker I feel like I'm asking for a favor"! This is very aligned to Tim's focus on the shift from transactions to relationship.

Digital transformation is an opportunity to transform the interactions. As most of the interactions are similar between banks, it has commoditized the service and those who differentiate the experience will stand out.

One example is the basic design of most of the bank websites, still based on a pull-down menu set, which treats everything with equal balance. This is Netscape from 25 years ago. That sort of logic, hasn't progressed in many applications. For ANZ we set the most common behaviors or interactions as the ones that you use most often, and delegated less frequent interactions to secondary visual real estate.

The problem is that the human interface has progressed enormously, by comparison. And so as a user, when you look at a set of offers all sorted with the same weight, whether it is 10 or 20 things in a pull-down menu, it reflects a lack of empathy and understanding for the way we can engage with technology today. It denies the clarity and simplification that should be there. It shouldn't be something where I have to set 25 preferences to personalize. If you look at most businesses in the financial sector in particular, there is a not a real focus on the user experience.

Q: How can they improve the digital customer experience? Have you worked on any digital customer experience projects that you can share with us?
We've been involved in a number of bank transformation programs that include the digital and physical touchpoints. We created a dynamic interface program for ANZ bank and created the Smart Banking program for Citibank. Both are in a transition to a better digital relationship with their customers. For digital user experience most systems focus on an equal weight for all transactions, services and interactions.

For the banking category the transition is really from the leadership through the touchpoint and support system design. The industry today is in transition and successful leaders who create user-centered experience are often promoted to the top levels of the company.

Not many banks focus on the value creation possible by designing human experience. What made Apple great was that Steve set the customer experience benchmark. If he felt that whatever was being delivered, wasn't being provided in a way that mattered to people, he would kill it. Most banks, I would say, initially look at it first from an economic perspective. What is the cost to do this, versus what is the value created from the action. Whether or not there's a short-term gain on that particular behavior, rather than understanding the long-term benefit of building people relations. It is a shift in mindset, from transactions to relationships. Business motivations tend to focus on short-term incentives and KPI's. The relationship value is therefore not the focus and is perhaps somewhat harder to quantify. But ultimately that is the difference between running a great company and an ordinary one.

Q: How do you define value on customer experience that a company can see? How can experience be quantified?
Great experience can create both short and long term benefits. One way to quantify the value is to look at it in the way the performance of customer-centric companies have done financially. In addition to sales or conversion success, advocacy becomes an incredible value. Companies who successfully deliver relevant, positive, emotionally-connected experiences outperform competitors by 6x, and receive 12x the loyalty and advocacy by being companies that people love and admire. Is it revenue, profit, loyalty, advocacy, growth, share value?

Metrics that quantify the benefits of great user experience are similar to ones that quantify successful businesses. If you look at all the possible companies/brands out there, I can point you to brands that we worked with. Virgin is a good example. Also Keep, Lincoln and Xiaomi in China. These are companies whose leaders people feel are doing things that matter for them, and they have created incredibly loyal and passionate customers. They tend to have customers who are very dedicated to the brand. If you can continue to deliver great products through that experience model, your business is going to be better.

When we started with Apple it was a $2.5 billion company. In August 2018 it became the first company to break the $1 Trillion valuation. There were a lot of people saying, when we designed the retail program, that it would be a colossal mistake for Apple to do the retail program. Some were saying the $10 million or whatever it was in the initial retail program should have been given to the shareholders. There was a lot of noise in the system because Apple was doing something that wasn't done by anyone else.

Value creation is when people adopt something. The difference between the original social media companies and Facebook was a better user experience. Facebook was trusted to create a better experience. Facebook was successful because people adopted it. Facebook, like all companies, will become less valuable if they erode the trust people put into the experience with the company. The metrics to be looking at are ones that define companies that people want to be a part of, want to be connected to. Today it's because the value systems of those companies are companies whose leaders people feel are doing things are relevant.

Many leaders are looking too closely at competing for this month's or this week's or this quarter's financials, so they don't spend the time or energy focusing on the things that will ultimately make their company strong.

Q: They are looking at the wrong metrics and they are looking for a short gain. So, basically, it should be a part of their long-term strategy. Right?
Warren Buffet says "never buy a stock you would not own for 10 years". The polarity of short versus long term gain is a bit of a trap. Shareholders look at short term value but smart ones look at longer time horizons and the creation of value. The focus on the human outcomes will lead to the desired business outcomes. Unfortunately, a typical business structure will be based on the near-term performance and that will influence decisions that may not be in the best interest of the customer experience. I think this tends to force companies to look at their feet, when they need to be looking at a longer horizon.

Q: Can you tell us about the smart banking project you worked on for Citibank?
When we started this there were many business metrics. They were trending down on innovation, trending down on relevance, trending down on personal service and innovation. All of these core bank services were in a steep 45-degree dive. Their business was not performing as well, because the model itself was based on an old paper-based world.

Citi in the retail banking space had never stepped back and looked holistically at how to transform what they were offering. Their program for that was a shift towards much stronger digital engagement. The ecosystem and the different touchpoints the branches have reflect the posture that banks have with their customers. Our strategy was to change the posture and change the relationship to the company. Ultimately, we built for customer experience and satisfaction. They went from 57th in customer satisfaction in the market to first. When they placed first in customer satisfaction after one year they were shocked. It ultimately reflected what a flat line banking customer experience was to move that much. The two businesses that consistently struggle with customer experience ratings are **banking and automobile dealerships.**

Banking and automobile dealerships. I think people dread engaging with banks and car dealerships because they are things we feel strongly about yet the experience is set up to be almost exclusively transactional. There is a disconnect between our emotional engagement and the experience we have offered to us. Our perception in both experiences it is usually that we don't matter as a person. The bank or the car dealership is predominately interested in our money and there is no sense of relationship or personal connection. The bank, car dealership, or electric company that figures out how to connect and establish a truly meaningful relationship with us will redefine their industry. This holds for all companies and organizations; those that can establish a meaningful relationship with their customers, clients or members, will be perceived as adding value and therefore will be rewarded with a premium based on loyalty and engagement.

These are two experiences the customers usually dread having. The psychological response to both of those categories is overwhelmingly negative. To me, those are the ones that are easiest to fix. The problem is getting around some of the category limitations within a bank or within a dealership, and starting to change those engagement models.

Again, if you focus on a valuable relationship, you tend to work around a lot of the typical tactical things, the typical hurdles that get thrown in the way, things like regulations. These are the common reasons people give for not providing a pleasant experience but are just an excuse for lack of effort.

Q: This is a radical re-design involving a considerable investment in the latest interactive and information technology. What lessons from your experiences would you say best apply to what others need to accomplish, and how would you persuade executives that these will pay off?
Building a new customer experience required Citibank to modularize their technology platform, build new touchpoints specific to the customer's mode of living, create a palette of applications, and provide the customer with the tools they need. The Citibank user interface is an integral part of the smart banking approach, conceived to make banking more relevant by bringing simplicity, ease-of-use and personalization, but it is just a start.

Is it worth it? To persuade executives or others stakeholders would depend on the metrics they are looking to achieve in their individual businesses. There are many ways to define return on experience. Here are a few:

Sales, Brand Awareness and Loyalty:
Apple: Valued at $2.5 billion in 1997 when we began. Today valued at $880B.

Customer Satisfaction, Brand Perception and Revenue:
2010 Citibank Japan was ranked #1 in customer satisfaction (up from #57). They have double the customer acquisition, and revenue is up 400%.

Foot Traffic and Shares:
Nissan: Previously 3,000 visitors per month. After completion, one million visitors came through the store during the first four months.

Market Share and Business Transformation:
Globe: The #3 telco in the Philippines with a 23% market share now has a 56% market share and is now the #1 Philippine Content Creation Company now.

Growth, Advocacy, Sales and Word of Mouth:
Lincoln: Launched November 2014 and by May 2015 Lincoln posted the most Lincoln cars sold in a month in Lincoln history. In 2016, Lincoln China dealerships ranked #1, #2 and #3 (performance) globally. In 2016, Lincoln was ranked as the #3 luxury automobile brand in China.

Growth, Brand Value, Innovation, and Relevance:
Xiaomi: 1-x increase in sales recorded with 100x increase in customer touchpoints (receptors) and ability to better define the products and experience (intelligence, see diagram on next page).

An idea alone is not innovation. Things that focus on human outcomes tend to lead to adoption if designed well. Adoption is the goal if you are looking to define innovation and value creation.

Notre Dame Proposal, Paris, 2019

How Matters

If you need to choose between beauty and function, what will you choose? I choose a better human outcome.

Notre Dame Proposal, Paris, 2019

Notre Dame Proposal, Paris, 2019

Notre Dame Proposal, Paris, 2019

Notre Dame Proposal, Paris, 2019

Polaris Packaging, 2014

POLARIS
ENGINEERED ACCESSORIES
LIGHTING
12: LED Light Bar
- 9.5-watt LED's produce 2,100 lumens
- Provides 1.5 times more light than the stock headlights
- Weather proof connectors with plug-n-play harness
- Extruded 6061 aluminum housing, with stainless steel hardware
- Includes custom lens spotlight/floodlight combination
50'
40'
30'
20'
10'
2,100
Lm

Polaris Brand Book, 2014

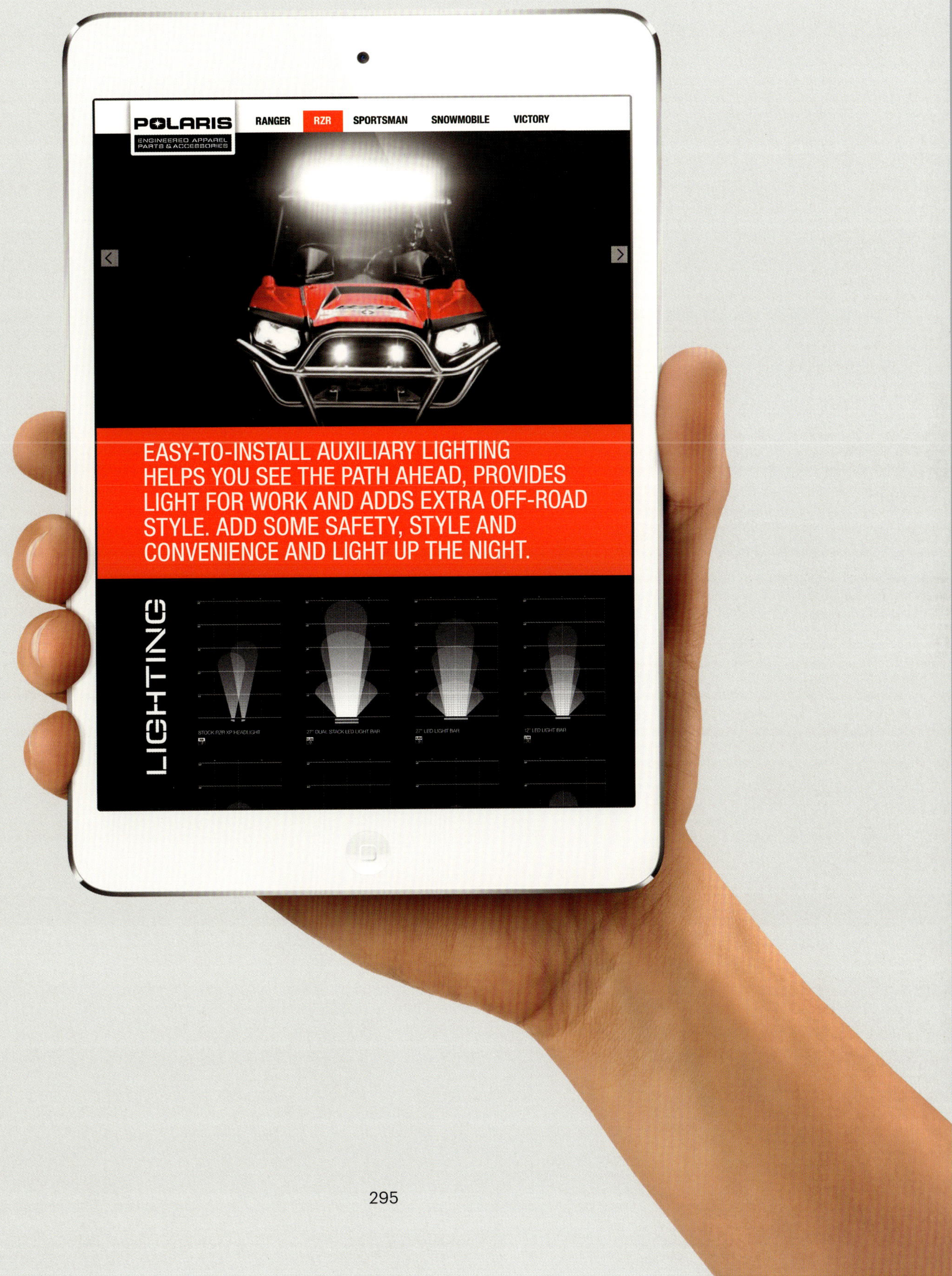
POLARIS
ENGINEERED APPAREL
PARTS & ACCESSORIES
RANGER
RZR
SPORTSMAN
SNOWMOBILE
VICTORY
EASY-TO-INSTALL AUXILIARY LIGHTING HELPS YOU SEE THE PATH AHEAD, PROVIDES LIGHT FOR WORK AND ADDS EXTRA OFF-ROAD STYLE. ADD SOME SAFETY, STYLE AND CONVENIENCE AND LIGHT UP THE NIGHT.
LIGHTING

Felissimo Headquarters, Kobe, 2018

Felissimo Headquarters, Kobe, 2018

Felissimo Headquarters, Kobe, 2018

Felissimo Headquarters, Kobe, 2018

Guazi.com
Guazi.com
Guazi.com

Guazi Flagship Store, Chengdu, 2018

Guazi Flagship Store, Chengdu, 2018

Guazi Flagship Store, Chengdu, 2018

客休区
Lounge

Guazi Flagship Store, Chengdu, 2018

Guazi Flagship Store, Chengdu, 2018

Q: How matters?
If you want extraordinary business success, then design is not optional or a nice-to-have—it's essential. Great design leads to outcomes that lead to adoption. Look at the most important design Google has created: single search box. It's a simple, single rectangle. This is what separated the Google search experience from all others that preceded it. This made Google relevant. Search relevance was similar to the others. Ease of use was the differentiator. The design made Google essential. It is able to leverage that relevance into 5 products: search, Gmail, YouTube, maps etc.

Q: What is the significance of design innovation in technology?
The only way for the human condition to progress is through meaningfully designed solutions. New ways of doing things lead to new opportunities and some opportunities are adopted by people.

Google's most significant innovation is its most human-centric and its most valuable. There has not been much other meaningful human design work from technology companies. Engineering yes. Design no. Innovation by definition requires adoption, but you can get baseline adoption through function. Technological innovation may be useful in uncovering a new capability, but without the application of that capability, it will likely be less impactful on human progress. The most successful outcomes are through a combination of design and engineering.

Q: So "how" is fundamental to successful technology?
As technology is an extension of our capabilities, at a simplistic level it becomes an extension of our tools. At its most complex it becomes something that drives creativity and innovation opportunities. The significance comes through the human value it generates. Only adoption can validate innovation in technology. Technology without human application is a pursuit or an interest but not true innovation. This means the design can impart more than its functional aspirations. Loyalty and preference come from a combination of creating an incredible solution for things people need and an incredible design that allows people to engage with it. The way it manifests is frequently different. It becomes things that transform the way we do things, how we live and transforms behavioral norms.

The more products and services become alike, the more that emotional connection becomes the differentiator. The best brands today realize this and are working to distinguish themselves. Experience design is one of the best ways to connect on an emotional level.

Q: And "how" can create enormous value?
Today, successful design can achieve distinction and preference through offerings and engagements that build emotional value, passion, and advocacy for the brand. How you do something matters. What separates Amazon, Facebook, Apple, or Google from others? Google was not the first or best search engine. When something is designed well, it can create incredible value. Great design today is more powerful than ever. Ensuring the experience can be communicated and appreciated has compound value in the touchpoints with the company.

The competitive advantage of transformative solutions is one thing. Groundbreaking experience creates an impact. When something has numerous receptors and garners valuable intelligence or insights, then loyalty, value and preference can create extraordinary human outcomes and business outcomes. If how matters, then design matters. Loyalty and preference come from a combination of creating an incredible solution for things people need and an incredible design that allows people to engage with it. Successful companies over time have had vital leadership who could connect the people and their offerings in meaningful ways.

Q: What about companies that are not design centric?
The shift is still not fully appreciated across all businesses. Companies like Alphabet (Google) are an interesting study because by most accounts the only significant revenue source is built on its most human-centric product—arguably its best-designed product—the single text search box. It can afford to experiment and develop the next great technology, but there is also a risk. As a business focused on engineering, the real value creation has happened with one great design solution. The single search box was the primary differentiator Google has from its competitors because it was more focused on better user experience. That solution drove adoption and adoption has driven revenue from

advertising. This seems to account for 90% of the revenue and other "bets" seem to struggle with user application and adoption. It is not an either-or situation. It should be a balance of great human-centric design and amazing engineering. I see unbalanced development like this in many companies. The technology can be profound if the human value is the driving force. Otherwise, it's a good experiment but cannot reasonably rise to the level of human innovation.

Q: Do you believe that the recipe that has brought you success is limited to major brands exclusively?
I would not refer to an approach to a **creative process as a recipe.**

Creative process as a recipe. One of the main reasons why the experience design approach that Tim is talking about is successful across industries from large multinationals to small SMEs, family businesses or start-ups is that the focus is on the human relationship. That relationship is such a fundamental need that we as humans have; to be connected in order to feel valued and appreciated.

Psychologically we then feel that there is a very unique bond and connection established. Based on this perspective it makes good sense that experience design is not just limited to companies and commercial applications but also governments, nonprofits, academic institutions. I have recently worked with a religious institution that was looking for ways to expand their "customer experience" based on establishing a meaningful relationship and therefore a psychological connection with their members.

It is not quite the right analogy as the term implies a formulaic approach to achieve a consistently reliable result. To deliver a consistently reliable result, it cannot be a one-size-fits -ll approach. Each process includes looking through a framework of investigation and applying creativity to arrive at an appropriate design result. Each business has similarities to others but they are never the same. The approach is applicable to not only major brands but SMEs or start-up businesses. We have undertaken work redesigning education processes and have looked at re-designing for governments and non-profits. The approach defines constraints and strategic opportunities to have an impact and support the client's desired outcomes

Q: Is there a connection to a company's success and their creative process?
Most companies change in order to remain competitive and to de-risk their business from the competition. Most companies will be challenged to maintain a successful innovation program without understanding the creative process and being able to manage creative teams either internally or externally. To innovate only under stress is remarkably risky for a company.

Q: You have a history of working at the intersection of technology, focusing on designing for human outcomes. What are key things that technology is providing and what are the risks?
Design is what makes technology meaningful for people, if done well. What is technological progress without human value? The biggest risk to technology is missing the focus on creating better outcomes for people. We know there will be disruption, but if we only focus on the thing, we will miss the why.

With the many emerging trends in technology—AI, robotics, etc.—the biggest challenge is how ato make technology more relevant. The most interesting challenge is watching design find its rightful place in relation to technological progress. This is the difference between say a Google glass and actual adoption. Technological factors were considered, but human design factors were not. A technological achievement, maybe, but not a success for people, and not a commercial success at all.

Q: What is the significance of design in technology?
The only way for the human condition to improve is through meaningful change. New ways of doing things lead to new opportunities, but only some opportunities are adopted and, in the best case, loved by people. Technological progress only happens when its application is relevant and has value. What it does for people is at the essence of its value as a technology.

Q: How would you suggest executives think about the benefits of this kind of data-centric customer experience re-design?

From research, the critical calculation of the return on investment (ROI) should likely include:

- Delivery on the human outcomes desired (NPS, and other feedback metrics) based on the clear definition of business values and human outcomes as a structural basis for the organization of the tasks, work streams, and individuals in a company.
- The value of additional, more timely and richer information about customer preferences, desires, feedback, and complaints. Synergies of combining product or service with necessary data and communications to support the most personalized offer on the operations side.
- Comprehensive analysis of potential efficiencies across the full range of systems: from savings in labor, time, and weight, for example.

Q: You have three offices today in China. Do you think design for Chinese companies and the design for international brands is similar? What are the differences?

A few years ago, the international brands wanted to enter China to compete with Chinese local brands. Now, many Chinese brands are not only competing more intently nationally, but looking to establish themselves in markets outside of China and to define themselves in the global marketplace. We are seeing incredibly competitive conditions in China, both with internal companies in a single category but also to be positioned as a top brand in the world. The primary shift has been in the nature of competitiveness in the market compared to a few years ago.

Q: Where would you say is the focus of your business today? Is it in Asia? North America? Europe or Middle East?

Rather than focus on geography, we prefer to focus on relationships with incredible people. It's where there is an opportunity to have an impact. The focus of our business has always been to be where the greatest opportunities for innovation are. Historically that was with Steve Jobs and Richard Branson's Virgin Atlantic Airlines. Our offices are in most major markets in the world today, but we keep a small presence in each and look to focus on the best opportunities.

Today, the Asian and India regions offer an incredible opportunity to have a global impact in many spaces. More than half of our offices are in this region as is half of the global population. Our belief in design to achieve remarkable human outcomes positions us perfectly to apply our expertise to benefit the greatest number of people. And I think the notion that design can have a remarkable impact on human outcomes means that we can work in regions that offer a potential to impact on the greatest number of people. There is an attractiveness to the ambition and the character of the people that we work with. We are excited by the boldness yet humble character of people who are the next generation of change agents in these locations.

Q: Can you share a project to make the case for experience design in China?
We have completed a number of programs in China in the past few years: Xiaomi (the electronics brand), Xiao Guan Cha (China's largest tea brand), Guazi (automotive), Anta (China's largest sportswear brand), and others. We designed the Lincoln Way for the Lincoln brand in China and transformed their place in the automotive category but Xiaomi is probably one of our most noteworthy there.

Q: The Chinese electronics company Xiaomi is well known in China. How did you know of Xiaomi? What was your impression of Xiaomi at the time?
We have been working in Asia on strategic projects for a long time. We observed the growth and the leapfrog approach to technology occurring in Asia. I became aware of Xiaomi initially through the relationship with the design team. We share a common background in our training and education from the Art Center College of Design in California. Xiaomi has a deep belief in design and the user experience. This was my introduction to Bin Lin, the president of the company.

They also have a remarkable background in software, based on founder Le Jun's success in that space, and with the leadership model, a unique structure for collaboration in multiple business sectors. My initial impression was that Xiaomi possessed a unique passion and exuberance—a youthfulness. It reminded me of an early Apple in some ways, which was their initial inspiration. But Le Jun and Bin Lin and the other founders, have a broad vision that was not the usual approach.

Q: Eight Inc. has been working globally for many years and growing quickly in Asia. What changes do you see in China? Which of your projects in China are you particularly proud of?
We have been focusing on growing our business relationships and clients here since 2010 when I relocated from San Francisco to Singapore. The most interesting aspect is the rapid change as we observe the differences in perception and development of technology.

Today, a majority of all smartphone usage is in Asia. As Asia is a mobile-first market, websites and hard lines are less relevant, and application design is prioritized and done with a completely different approach. As the ecosystems are fundamentally different, these companies have developed entirely different rules of engagement.

This is fundamentally different from the Western progression of technology of fixed landlines and browsers. The application design approach in Asia has been to become aggregators rather than specialists in individual applications. To essentially leapfrog the western approach. Initially most were simply Western lookalikes. Today that is very different. The west has single function apps, while in Asia apps are more multi-functioning. The design is competing as more lifestyle platforms that deliver chat, call, banking, taxis, video, and exchange. Asian apps could be less user restrictive and consolidated, with an expanded breadth of language to compete more broadly but still under the broader Chinese governmental controls and objectives.

Regarding our work in this region, I am most happy that all our projects that have resonated with people in a market, bringing both Western businesses to China and Chinese businesses to the Chinese market. The next push is connecting Chinese brands to global markets. It is really not about the nation but to support the people who are making better things for others. Competition is a good thing.

Our work for Lincoln China is their most successful retail program in the world. A distinct experience rooted in the Lincoln core brand attributes while being relevant to the Chinese people in ways other luxury car companies have never been. The Lincoln China program has now become the new Lincoln global program.

Our Xiao Guan Cha design elevates Chinese tea to a new standard of excellence while respecting the craft and care that is behind every serving of this healthy and culturally significant product. This program is rapidly becoming the leading Chinese tea experience and the premium tea product in China.

With Xiaomi, the most interesting part is the company strategy inverting the relationship between great design and accessibility for the most people—the opposite of the traditional luxury market structure. I believe this company may possess the capacity to disrupt the global market in ways that the some of the Korean businesses have disrupted Japanese manufacturing, for example.

Q: In the last few years, Xiaomi has changed a lot. It all started in 2012 and five years later Xiaomi has already became an enormous company with over $100 billion in revenue. What's your impression on the Xiaomi brand?
I think Xiaomi is one of the most interesting companies from China. It clearly has the design and engineering ability to bring world-class design excellence to a vast number of people. The traditional model has always been sorted around the highest design qualities being the most expensive, therefore limiting the number of people who could afford these goods. By positioning high-quality design products further down the pricing pyramid, Xiaomi stands to improve more people's lives but also has access to a much broader market. Initially, the focus was more on a comparison brand with Apple in China but as the company has matured the product offerings have expanded.

Q: As e-commerce continues to boom, what role do stores play for retailers today?
Scott Galloway accurately predicted the death of pure-play retailers in 2015 just prior to Amazon acquiring Whole Foods. Last mile is still their challenge. Pure-play e-commerce's role is shifting; to compete in one channel with the likes of Amazon is very difficult without other customer touchpoints. Interestingly, stores are also as vital as they've ever been, if done well. When you look at retail today, good retail is not suffering, bad retail is. I'm talking about the people who haven't decided to be competitive or work on solutions that impact the end-user experience, or to integrate with technology versus seeing it as a competing channel. It's a sorting out of the market. If you compare in America the number of stores per person to other parts of the world, we're something like ten times more saturated. In a way, I think it's a natural evolution of overabundance, but I think those who are more digitally savvy are those that are going to succeed rather than those who ride the old model into the ground.

Q: Eight Inc. promises to design "meaningful human experiences." What role does technology play in that?
The majority of sales start in digital space prior to physical. Content is becoming stronger in building your relationships. It's about making sure you're creating deeper meaning. Technology is just a tool to get to that. It's a question of the outcome as the primary objective and then you use the right tool to achieve that outcome. It's not about just checking the box and getting the latest technology. It's one of those things where you have to be consistently evaluating what the human outcome is to have the business outcome. Building content that intersects with commerce is potentially the holy grail. Great content drives conversion rates, engagement . It used to be about mindshare. Today, it's not just share of mind but share of emotion.

Q: Do you think the way retailers look at their brick-and-mortar spaces has changed?
Yes, absolutely. What the Apple work helped develop was making the store a brand touchpoint that could convey aspects of the brand that were previously left to a communications role. It is also a receptor. You can feel who and what the Apple brand is by the experience you have in the space. Now more companies see their stores as touchpoints rather than just a transaction spaces—points for an exchange of information, goods, and services. Not only the store experience but the content and commerce relationship is becoming more critical and integrated. Essentially a multi-emotion engagement through content is delivering the strongest relationships and the higher sales.

Q: Some companies are taking that idea to an extreme, and choosing not to sell any products at their stores. What do you make of that?
I don't believe you can just be an experience store without offering something meaningful. A few have tried it, but the idea that you could do a brand store and not attribute any other values to it is a tough one for some companies to make work. The store is the point where it's possible to drive the highest emotional connections, and we know that tends to drive the most conversions. If you're creating that emotional environment and not doing a conversion, then you're likely wasting that opportunity. We are more of a proponent of what we call a Mono-channel or Live-channel strategy that extends the value of that opportunity.

Q: How might the role of the store change in the future?
I think retail is a very interesting barometer. It's one of the business categories where if you're not refreshing your offer every five years you're probably behind your competition. A lot of companies that haven't been looking at disrupting themselves end up being beaten by someone who is. Retail is exceptionally competitive, especially challenging. And I think it's quite complicated when you think about the human psychology in addition to all the other functional parts that go into a thriving retail program. It is a leading indicator of how other businesses will remain relevant. The store will remain a touchpoint and great brands will do more than just exchange goods.

Q: For many years the term omni-channel has been used to define a retail ecosystem strategy. You recently discussed the difference between that and a Live-channel strategy?
Historically the omni-channel term has been used to define the idea that there would need to be both separate digital and physical channels to retail. This is a by-product of the growth occurring in different time-frames and a polarized view of retail channel types. This emerged from a natural additive growth of new channels for retail. The opportunity is that the adopters of the technology have changed behaviors. Most people remember a pre and post iPhone world. For digital natives have only known a post iPhone world. For them mobile engagement is like oxygen: it's only missed if they don't have it. For them it's less gizmo fascination, as it is with Millennial's, and more essential enablement. The idea of Live-channel retail assumes simultaneous channel engagement versus additive. The Xiaomi example that demonstrates the potential engagement of a simultaneous or Live-channel strategy.

Q: Eight Inc. created the term Live-channel. What strategy for experience design does this imply a new relationship with technology?
Our relationship with technology has always been in a state of evolution. A Live-channel strategy merely recognizes the current state of this relationship. Today we can exist simultaneously in both a physical world and a virtual or digital world. This addresses the shift from a series of independent channels or touchpoints to one that is simultaneously and seamlessly interconnected.

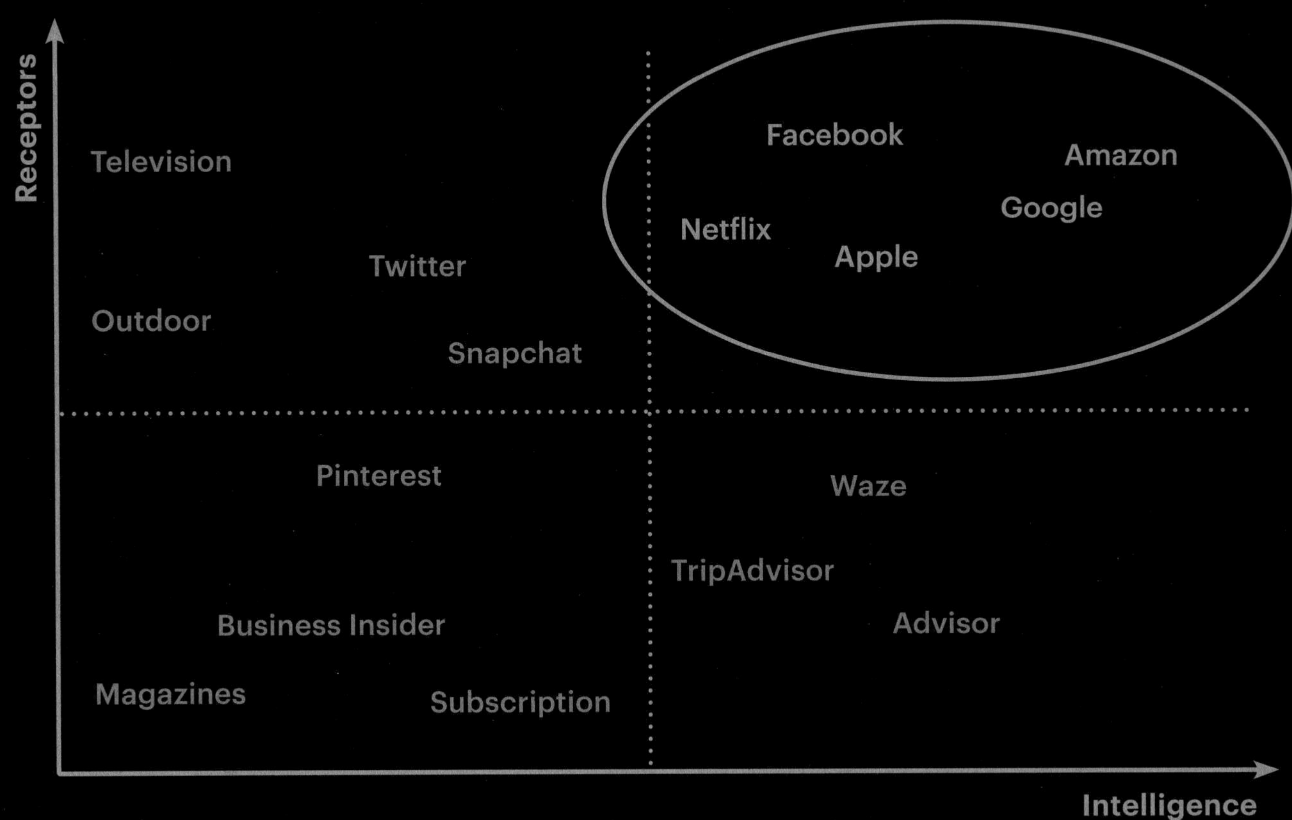

The New Algorithm of Value by Professor Scott Galloway,
Source: L2, 2017

Nam June Paik Museum, Seoul, 2004

Risk and Outcomes

Risk is both doing or not doing. Business is not static. Great design is often obvious in retrospect.

Nam June Paik Museum, Seoul, 2004

Nam June Paik Museum, Seoul, 2004

keepland
Keep线下运动空间

Keepland, Beijing, 2019

Keepland, Beijing, 2019

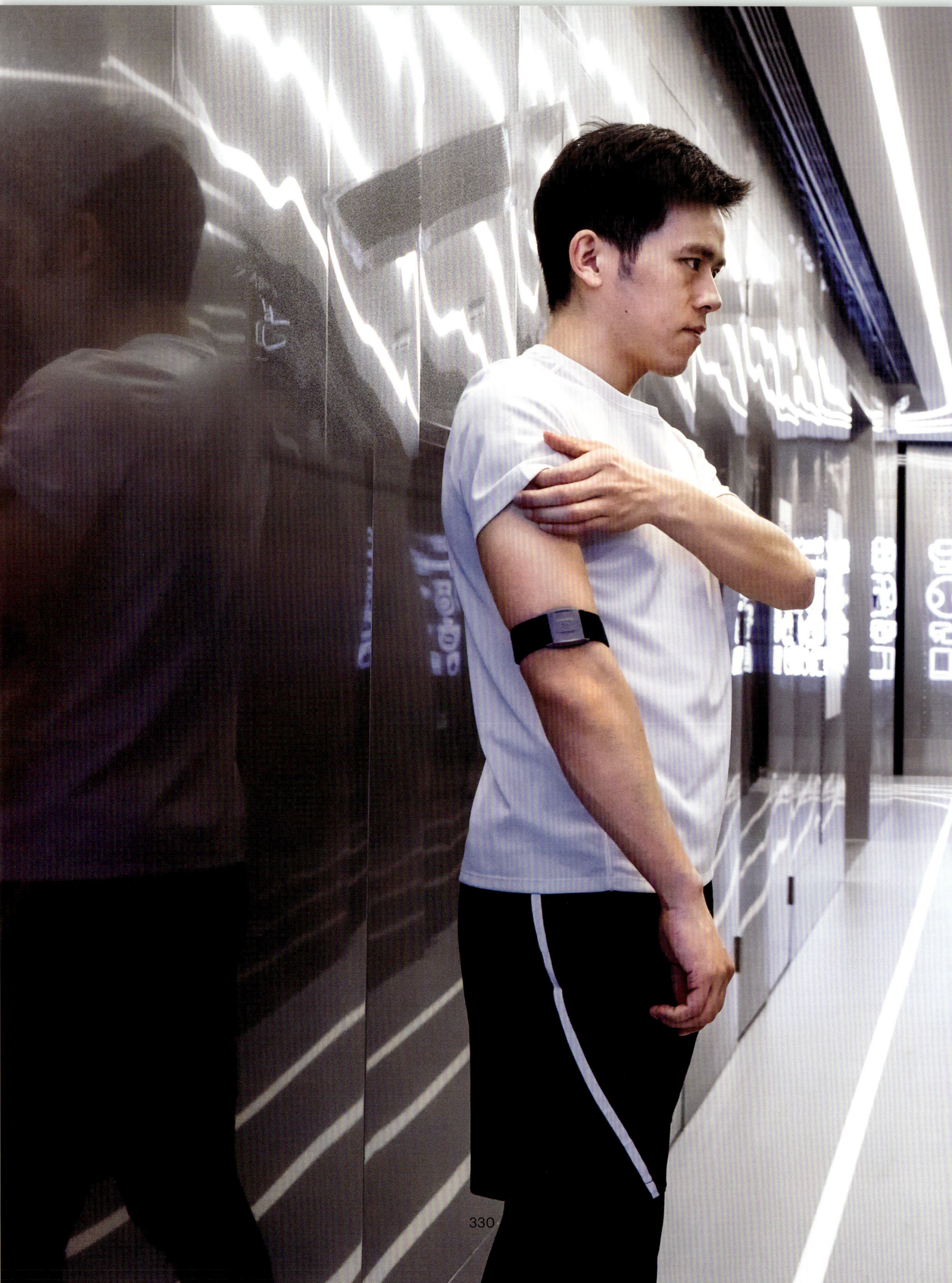

Keepland, Beijing, 2019

Storelli, New York, 2003

Storelli, New York, 2003

Suiki Lor Branding, San Francisco, 2016

SUIKI.

Suiki Lor Branding, San Francisco, 2016

Malama Learning Center, Hawaii, 2013

Malama Learning Center, Hawaii, 2013

Malama Learning Center, Hawaii, 2013

Edgewood Residence, Mill Valley 2003

Edgewood Residence, Mill Valley 2003

Q: According to Apple Insider, Apple spent approximately US $745m on design, construction, and leases for its first wave of retail stores. Within three years, Apple's stores surpassed US $1bn in annual sales —faster than any previous franchise.

Regarding value, Steve equated the store design and construction costs to the equivalent of a "rounding error." He was one of our few clients who had the value equation balanced to recognize the design value. When you look at the value created through the retail program and amazing products, you can see the channel costs are relatively insignificant. Brand-building, performance, and perception of value are where the revenue is generated. At almost any cost, it's expensive if poorly done, while cost is immaterial if well done. The Apple story demonstrates the revenue that can be generated by investing heavily in what are perceived as "softer" aspects of brand-building and the customer experience. It also proves that going against the current trend—Gateway was shutting down its single-brand retail operation while Apple was expanding into that exact space—can also prove a smart play.

Q: Being risk averse is a significant factor in business decisions. If design is about change, how do you reconcile risk with your clients?

People tend to see **risk in change.**

Risk in change. Indeed, risk is involved both in doing and not doing. The concept of the primary task within an organization engages the leadership team by asking the question "what is the work to be done" or "what is the task that we need to address". The primary risk is the risk of choosing the wrong task. Because of this, there is indeed this tension between doing and not doing which is created due to the anxiety that comes from the fear that one might choose the wrong task.

In Tim's example with the Apple Store, one could see that perhaps the primary task for Apple at the time was to take ownership of its brand and to differentiate itself in the market. As he notes, clearly there was a very strong risk involved in this decision as many "experts" in the market thought that this was a flawed decision. It is because of this risk that there are barriers to both innovation and creativity within all organizations. The task of the leader is to be able to identify and acknowledge this risk, involve others and be open to their opinions and to make an informed but nevertheless a calculated decision on the value of doing nothing versus the value of making the creative or innovative move.

The example of Steve Jobs and the Apple Store and especially his behavior the night before, shows clearly the role of the leader in identifying with the primary task and the primary risk. Steve was able to identify, acknowledge and, most importantly, to contain the anxiety caused by the uncertainty, of the decision. Clearly there was risk and that risk caused uncertainty and added to the risk was the general public opinion that this was a very bad strategic move for Apple.

And yet Steve identified the risk and then took the steps necessary to inform himself that this decision was indeed aligned with Apple's primary task, in terms of the brand's relationship with its customers. This enabled him to make a calculated guess that this alignment would be recognized, acknowledged and rewarded by the Apple customers. Such an approach does not remove the risk of making the wrong choice but it does greatly reduce the risk involved.

We see risk in both change as well as lack of change. Status quo is more comfortable and seemingly safer. Businesses today are more at risk than they may have ever been with technology. What seems obvious looking backwards was never that obvious initially. When you look at any design the solution must be thoughtful; not just looking at precedent but looking forward. It means putting a stake in the ground and making a commitment to a point of view. It is the basis of fear that leads to incremental design and insignificant design.

Few leaders create an environment where taking creative risk is safe. For disruptive work to be undertaken and explored. There are few great opportunities to create great work and it is critical for great design to be created through a collaboration of great client leaders and great design teams. Our desire is to look for the best opportunities to create meaningful design.

Q: Risk seems to always be a factor when you create something new. How do you convince clients that the new thing you are creating is worth the risk?

In most categories of work, changing from a solution that is commonly what your peers are creating is perceived as a risk. There is also a risk of doing nothing. In our architectural work, we have consistently pushed to focus on changing an industry standard when that standard creates a similar outcome to the competitors.

Businesses tend to run on numbers and the resulting calculations. But businesses that strive to be consumer-oriented, rather than commodities, ignore significant competitive advantage and do so at their peril. In making investment decisions, it is important always to assess "the cost of doing nothing." For airlines, investing in Wi-Fi, for example, when the time is right and the lessons of earlier attempts have been absorbed, is improving both their return on investment and their return on expectations—to the benefit of their customers and their business.

Q: Your architecture work has been influential in many categories. Do you see experience focus as driving the architectural solutions Eight Inc. has created?

When I was in my high school drafting class, my instructor told me that drawing is not the way to best understand architecture. He advised I travel to visit the great architecture in the world, to experience them, move through them, and to feel the effect of the structure and light. All of this was in order to better understand the intent and know why the forms and spaces created would imbue an experience for the occupant.

I think we approach architecture in a way that is counter initially to the way the majority of architecture is taught and practiced. Most architectural education focuses on form. We are looking for architecture that is based on the experience people have with the interaction of a building or environment.

We are looking to create a differentiated experience to build value in a project, particularly in a competitive environment. The two most fundamental aspects we look at above the base function requirements are related to what differentiates the human experience and builds better emotional connections with the experience. This is exactly what other successful architecture or design has accomplished by differentiating the human experience, and it definitely also built a better connection at the emotional experience level with its customers.

Most of the old ways of looking at creativity in architecture are a result of an architecture education system that is outdated due to limitations of how to visualize the experience. Computers have emulated the old technology (drafting and modeling) and often misplaced in its value.

Appropriately, education initially focused on basic functional objectives of construction and materials but often with the key differentiator based on the form of the building as an object. It was primarily done this way because these are the only tools we have used to teach architecture since the beginning of architecture. Architecture students are being taught to illustrate three-dimensional objects in two-dimensional space with modeling, either in physical or digital form, designed to extend the two-dimensional representation of the form to a three-dimensional representation. This leads to the objectifying of a building or design and moving away from creating value to perpetuating the ego of the architect.

Realistically, most great architecture is **appreciated** through the experience with it.

Appreciated. I think the struggle here is not uniquely limited to architecture but in fact to almost all aspects of education in which the tools are almost exclusively rational, causal and structural. Such tools and ways of addressing issues are closely aligned to the "left brain" approach to things. The experiential and interactional perspective approach with the task is much more based on the non-rational and associative processes that are more frequently associated with the "right brain" functions.

Much has to do with the sequence of an encounter, the movement through space, interactions with others, time of day, light and air, views and space, and how it fits into a cultural conversation.

These are all qualities that the architectural education system struggles to illustrate, therefore making the design of the experience difficult to explore. It is hard to develop better solutions when the only tools we have to understand them are limited to the form of the object.

This is where I struggle with the traditional "star" architect or designer. We tend to commoditize architecture in a culture as a consumable, and as an architect we strive for a form; a signature. Then, when someone commissions the work, the expectation is a repetition of a "style" of architecture. Sadly, for humanity, the most common focus is far more on the architect's ego than the user's experience.

Q: Is this approach appropriate for real estate projects?
Any real estate development project is about value creation—human value and, often, financial value. The challenge with architecture is, that becomes permanent, which is much different than an iPhone or other consumable products. Architecture transcends time and generations of people in many cases and is therefore far more complex to consider concerning experience.

Defining and building experience with a structure that becomes a place that other people want to be part of is ideal. If we are creating hospitality destinations or office complexes, each benefit from what we define as an experience master plan. If you look at a master plan for a city or a development, it typically organizes complex elements into a plan to ensure it works at a physical level. We create an Experience Master Plan (EXMP) to define how complex human outcomes are achieved across the environment, products and services, communications, and behavior experience realms. These ensure multiple user journeys, which are defined, and, more than just the physical attributes of a project being defined, provides guidelines so that the physical parts of the experience will lead to the desired outcomes for the project.

Q: You talk about incremental design. What do you mean by that?
It's a strategy and technique that evolved with the consumption society from the industrial era as a way to create incremental value. Industrial design led the way with incremental improvements offering little real value improvement. Today, real estate developers emulate each other's solutions, and ultimately what was a unique value can become common or diluted. To create value, there is a reward if you can improve the experience for people.

The most common example today is in technology: an incremental improvement on a feature, color, a dimension etc. We are living at a time where the most disruption and change is happening in technology, but there's also a tendency, particularly after Steve Jobs passing away, to go back to a world of incrementalism. Industrial era consumption "norms". In technology, it appears we are going back to a pre-Steve Jobs era. Most companies use technology as a justifier of progress. The premise that the technological capability is what defines progress is misguided. It's the application of the technology that makes it meaningful and enables human progress. That is actually technology.

No one notices 'quite'. People don't care much about things that do not add real value through the design of the experience. Companies can only do that for so long. People have to care about what the improvement is, about what impact the design and technology can make.

What it does for people. Design has a conscience (and some might say, a soul). It needs to serve a purpose and do some good, to transform the way we live. This is where principles play a huge part. Design has purpose. Obsess over experience, not just form and function. Make sure every detail is better than it needs to be, but with the understanding that superficial change is no change at all.

We must first understand what we define as creating value. Is it money? Is it the clients that we design great architecture or design for? Is it happiness for the people who experience those projects? Is it the fulfillment that we get as creators? I think we all inherently define our own answer to that question through what we buy or participate with. The notion that there are just a few people who can create innovation is not about capability but the correct alignment of the objectives. The individual is challenged today because of the complexity of the factors driving relevant experience. Teams accomplish this best as opposed to individuals. Incremental improvement is never defined as innovation except by marketers.

Q: If we look at value creation, what are the key ideas people should think about when creating something new?
I think there are a key elements to consider if one is looking to create value. Simon Sinek's Golden Circle says to start with "why?" To question why the product or company deserves to exist? It's also important to look for opportunities that may come from uncommon insights. Success also often requires courage. It must start with a focus on human outcomes, how to be simple, honest, relevant and connected. Ideally to avoid being incremental. Incremental destroys value. Ultimately, value creation is driven by people **adopting** what you offer.

Adopting. An important but often overlooked aspect of value creation is that, much like fairness, trust or credibility, value creation is something that you as an individual or an organization are unable to assign. Just as an individual cannot say "I have credibility" in that credibility is something that others ascribe to that person, it is equally impossible for an organization to say, "we're adding value". It is the market, the stakeholders, the customers or even the team who will determine whether or not your interactions and your decisions are value adding or value destroying. Every action, every decision is perceived by others as either adding value or destroying value. There is no neutral state.

Q: Why is Simon Sinek's Golden Circle important?
As he accurately identifies, "People don't buy what you do; they buy why you do it." Why matters. Why do or should people care about your beliefs or the purpose of your company. Who remembers the first iPod? Most people. This was a turning point for Apple. But there has been a gradual shift. When we think of products and technology today we tend to look at specifications and the technology: how thick it is, the speeds and feeds, etc. What is significant about the iPod is it represents real innovation, a different way of looking at what technology can do for people.

Does anyone remember how much memory the iPod had? Nobody. And nobody cares. It doesn't matter. All that people remember is 1,000 songs in your pocket. What matters is what it did for people, and that's how we should think about our products. While the third one was slightly better than the previous one, no one remembers or cares. So I think that it is a great example to start to reframe the questions that we ask ourselves when we design something. That way we don't start by looking at technical specifications, but instead understand purpose and meaning to help define the real value. What is the meaningful value of the things we're creating?

Q: Uncommon insights. How do you look at the research and insights?
Common insights are hardly **insights.**

Insights. The psychoanalyst and contemporary thinker Christopher Bollas refers to the "unthought known," that exists within our individual and collective unconscious and is waiting to be "discovered". That discovery occurs primarily through associative thinking rather than causal thinking. The associative thinking opens up the boundaries of thought thereby creating the space for the emergence of the "unthought known". There is a close connection between the "unthought known" and the idea of "not knowing what I don't know". The goal that we have is to use all means to surface the "unthought known" and those issues that we "don't know that we don't know".

To create value it often begins with uncommon insight. The information world has been flattened, we have a lot of common insights—probably more common that we would like to believe. Many clients complain they see the same presentations with the same Google images from many different designers. So how do we get uncommon insight?

I think one of those things that will help distinguish the work is when you begin to appreciate insights that people may have but may not be able to articulate. Human qualities that are inherent to a creative process and that make design something difficult to replace with formula, algorithm or artificial intelligence.

Human creativity requires skill, insights and emotional intelligence, and is based on the idea we have to be sensitive enough to see things that are unseen, and understand the differences between things that are driving human outcomes. Things that people may need but not be able to articulate.

Nike Zoom Lebron IV Launch, New York, 2007

Leading Creativity

"What planet are you guys from?" —Steve Jobs

Swatch Olympic Pavilion, Atlanta, 1996

Swatch Olympic Pavilion, Atlanta, 1996

Swatch Olympic Pavilion, Atlanta, 1996

Swatch Olympic Pavilion, Atlanta, 1996

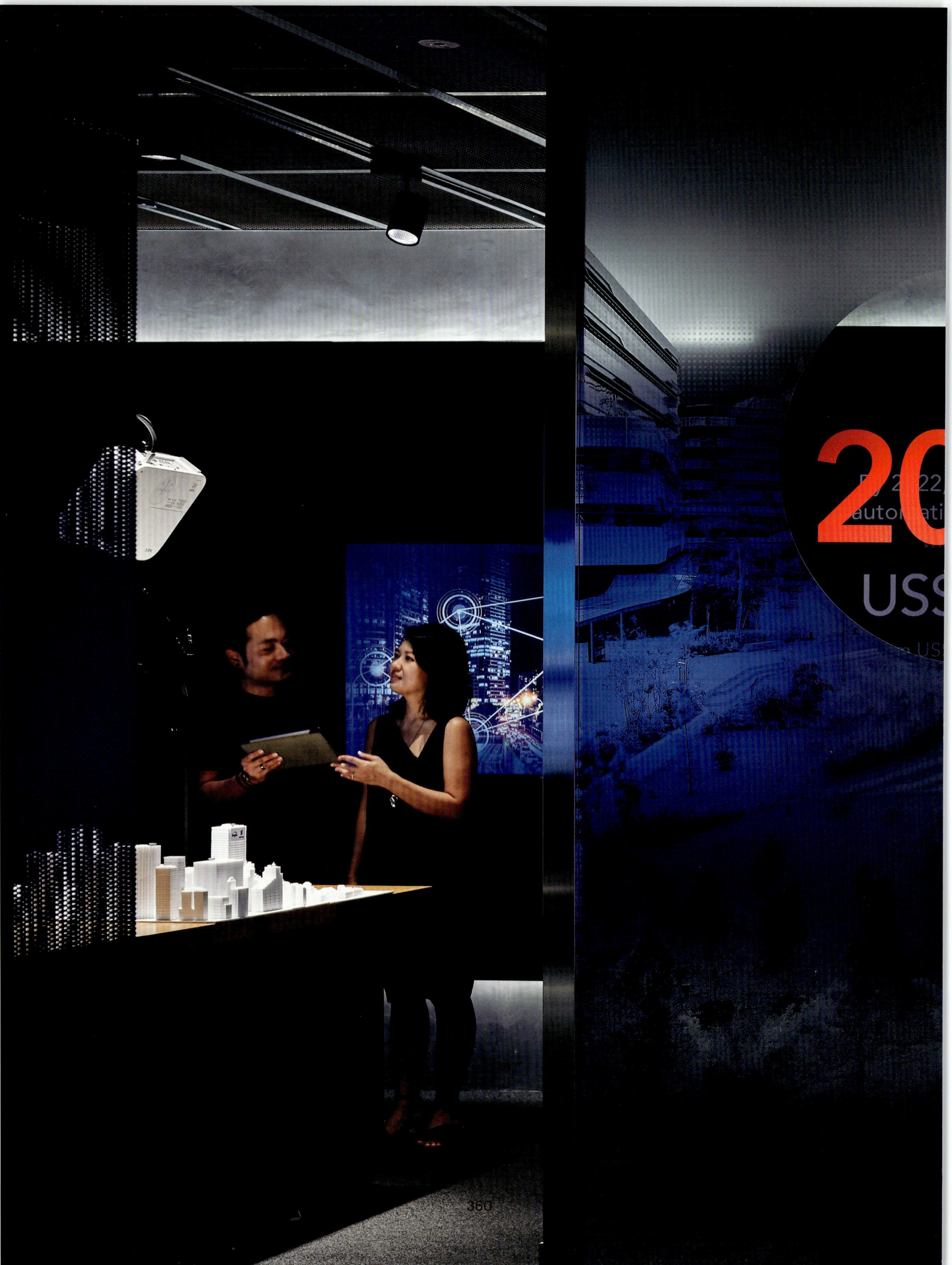

Singtel FutureNow, Singapore, 2019

Singtel FutureNow, Singapore, 2019

Singtel FutureNow, Singapore, 2019

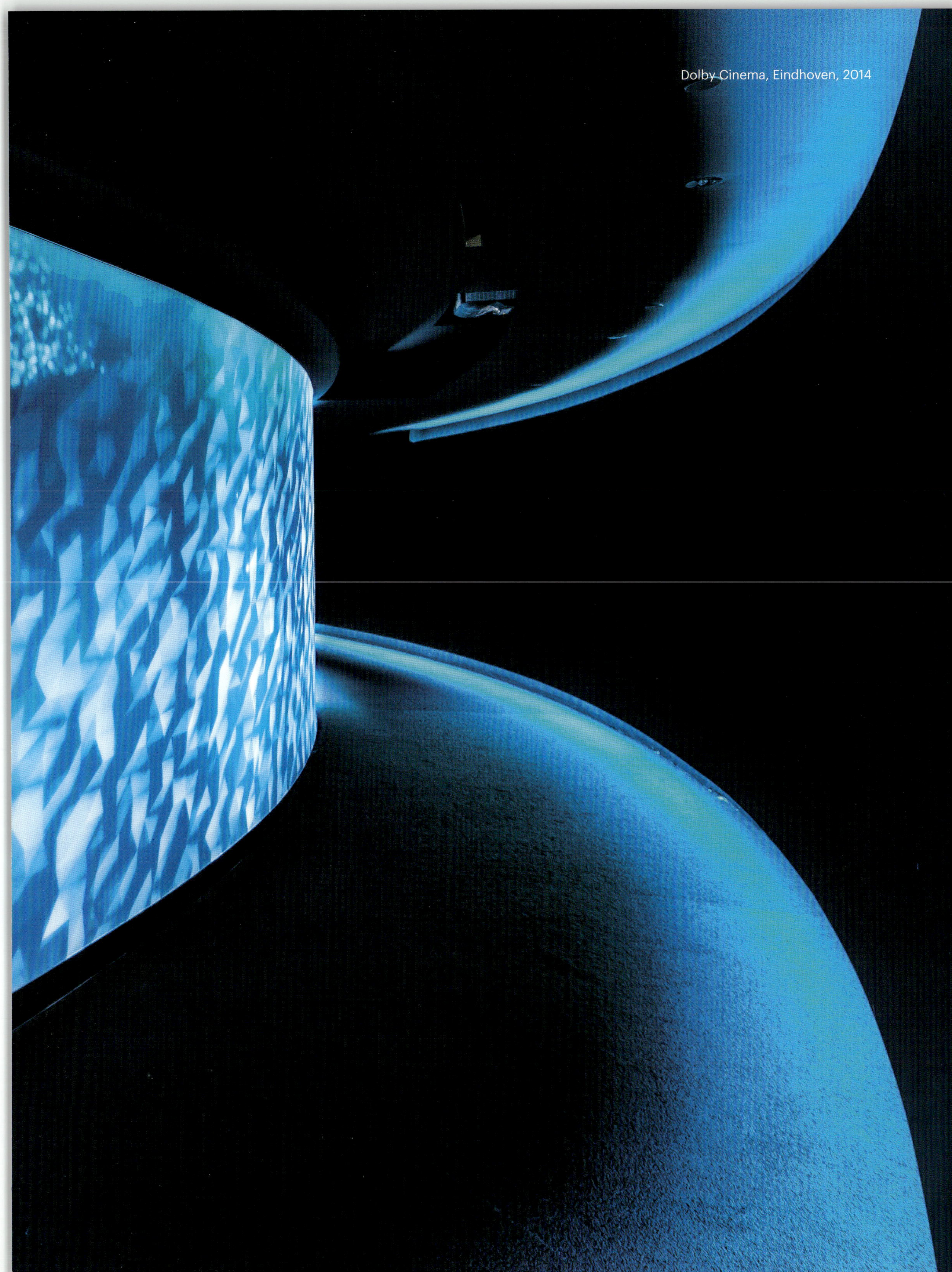

Dolby Cinema, Eindhoven, 2014

Dolby Cinema, Eindhoven, 2014

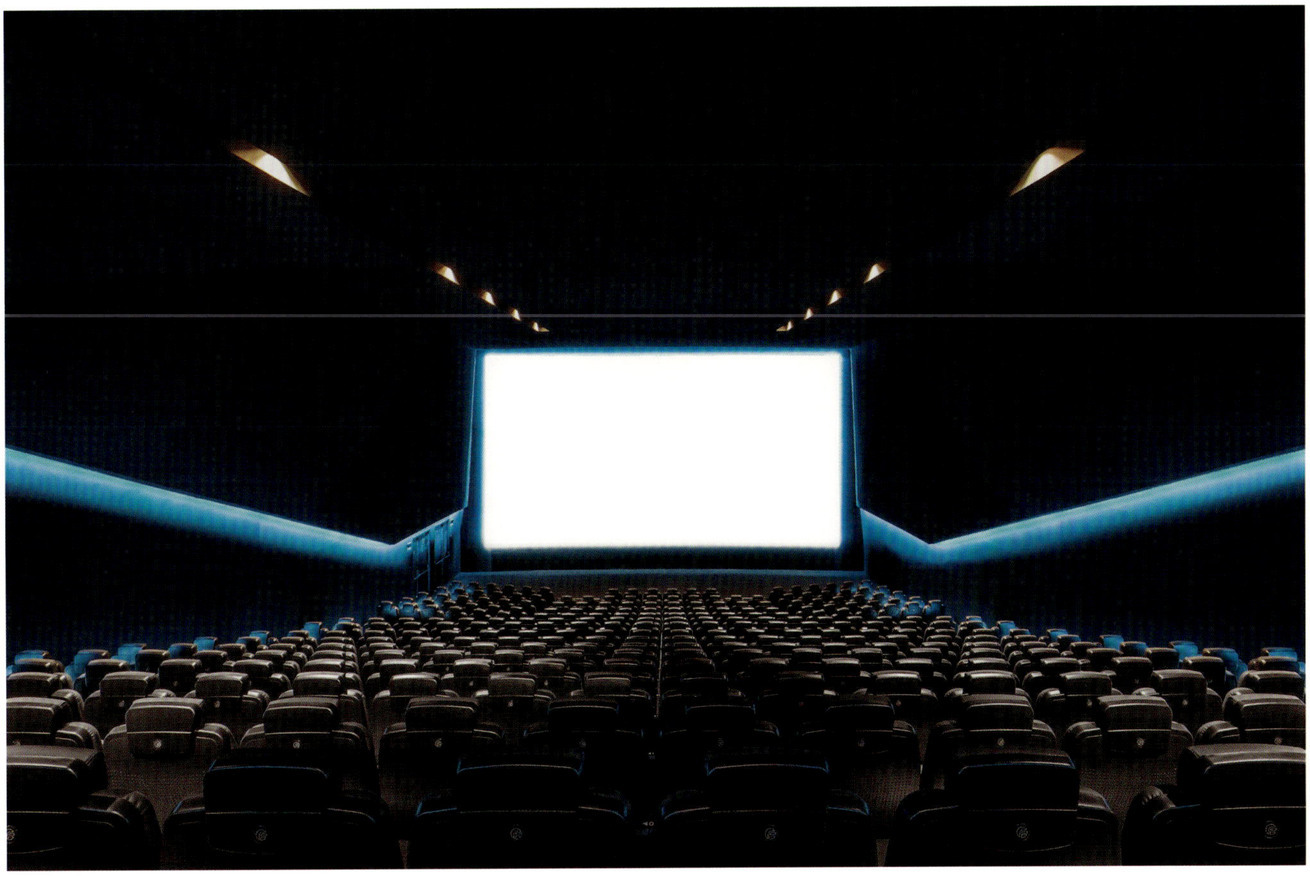

Dolby Cinema, Eindhoven, 2014

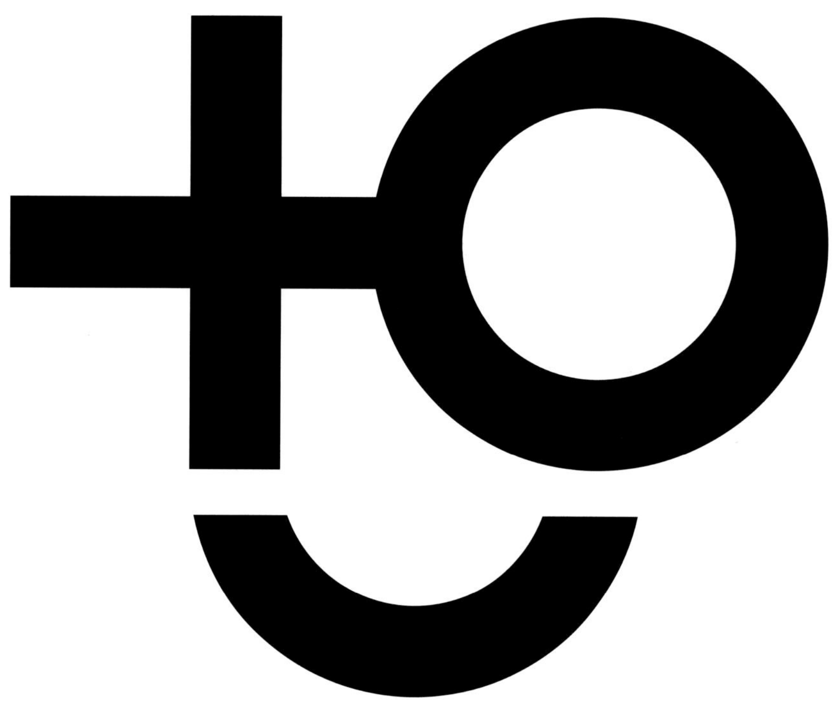

Tomorowww, Global, 2015

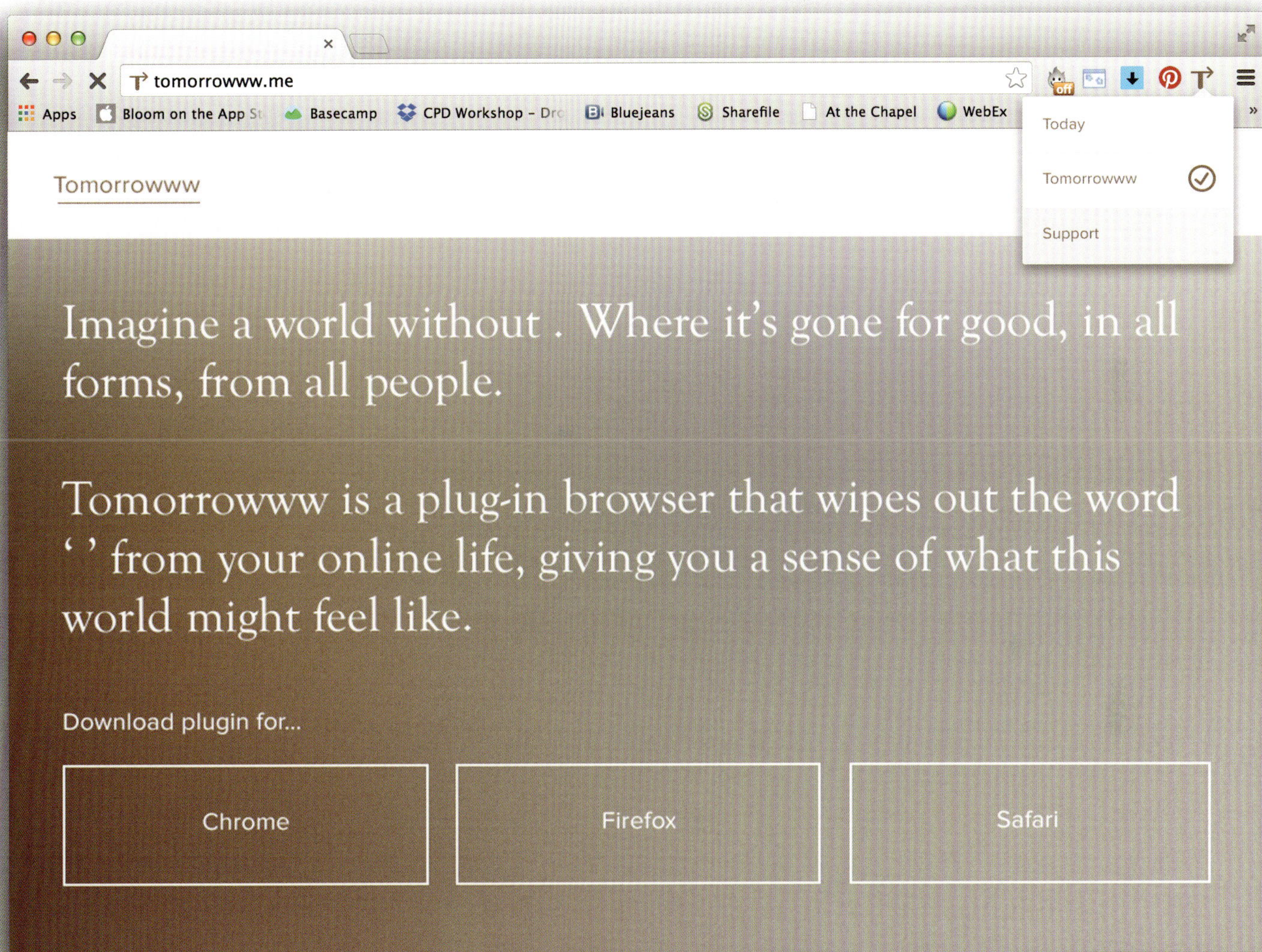

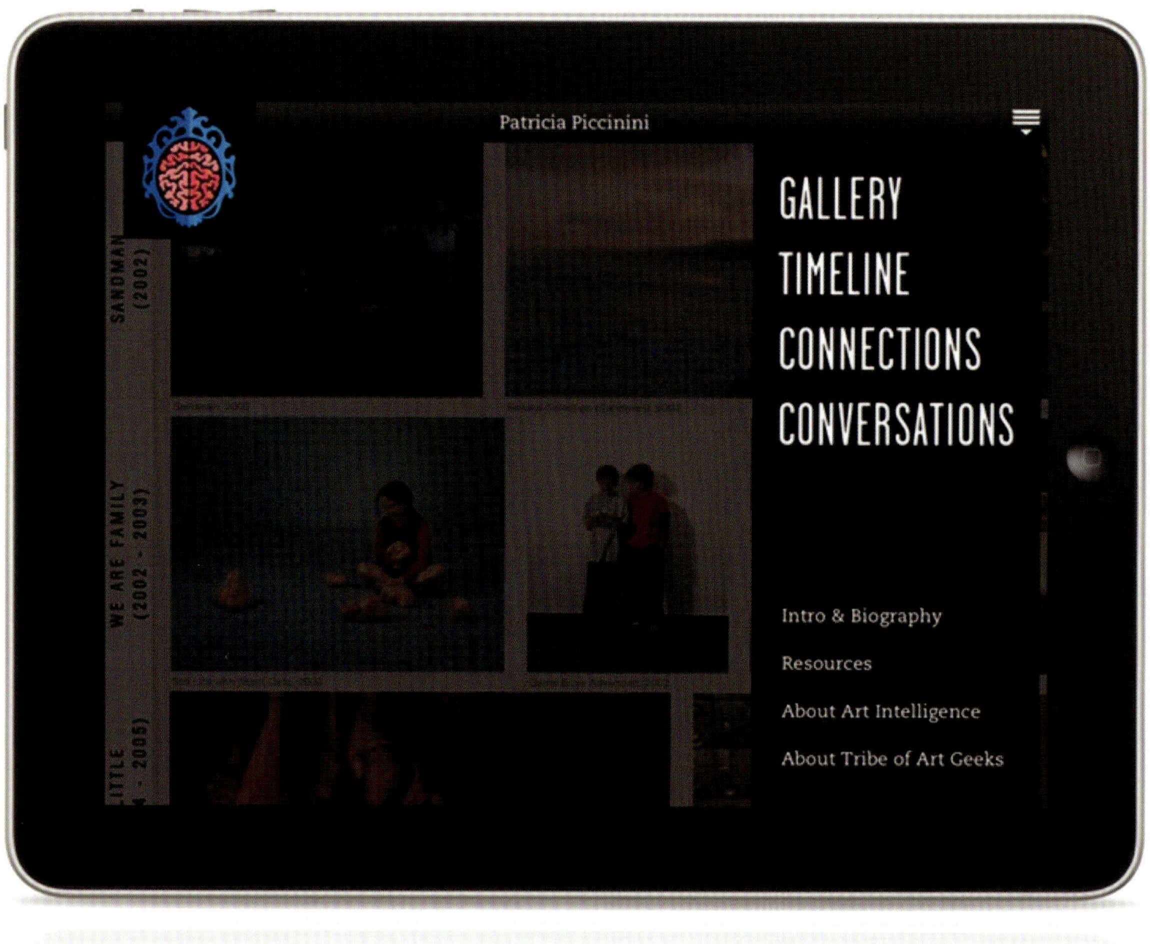

Art Intelligence, Global, 2012

Art Intelligence, Global, 2012

Guazi Headquarter Office, Beijing, 2018

DonorsChoose.org, New York, 2014

DonorsChoose.org, New York, 2014

INSEAD Creative Garage, Singapore, 2016

Q: What are the challenges you see working with creative people?
Creativity is one of the most powerful tools a company has and probably the least understood. The creative process is nonlinear and relatively inefficient. To be appropriately harnessed, teams need to have leadership that can follow the proper way to construct creative opportunities, and attract creative thinkers and doers. Most critically it requires a framework to align with the objectives of human outcomes, and insights into what will add value to the outcomes.

Q: How are today's business leaders equipped to lead creative teams?
Programs such as the INSEAD program integrated with Art Center College of Design, The Stanford Business program and the D-School are offering process and case study examples. Fundamentally business must provide a safe environment for exploration. It is a matter of connecting theory and application. Not just the insights but ultimately the design through the delivery of the solution. It requires skill in selecting which things to pursue and which not to. Without a focus on the human outcomes, the choices become blurred, and delivery becomes more of a challenge. It becomes critical for a business to be cultivating an environment to enable creativity and driving it through the organization.

Leadership is a key as well, to set the context for success.

Leadership. At INSEAD we work extensively with leaders in terms of helping them understand first of all themselves and then their teams and organizations with respect to change and the various factors that contribute to making change a difficult process which is often unsuccessful. When we speak about creative teams and innovation we're speaking about change. Leaders who have a psychological understanding of themselves as well as of how to lead teams and organizations during change will be much more effective in also facilitating creativity and innovation.

The environment that Tim speaks about is very much related to the concept of psychological safety (Amy Edmondson, *The Fearless Organization: Creating Psychological Safety in the Workplace for Learning, Innovation and Growth*, 2018) which is the responsibility of the leader. It refers to creating a situation within a team and the organization where all individuals feel that it is safe to express their ideas and thoughts without being concerned that they will be, in one way or another, negatively sanctioned or criticized or even made fun of as a result of their contribution or their idea. We find that in situations in which the leader has been able to create psychological safety and the space for associative thinking (which is often the birthplace of creativity and innovation) that creativity is almost inevitable. Almost everyone in the organization has "interesting ideas" or creative contributions but they are reluctant to speak up for fear of being in one way or another negatively impacted.

Because so much about creating a creative space in an organization is about leadership, it's also important to look at the recent work coming out of MIT (Deborah Ancona & Hal Gregersen, *Problem-Led Leadership: An MIT Style of Leading*, MIT Management, Sloan School, October 2017) in terms of "problem led leadership". They found that MIT graduates don't see being a leader as a top priority. In fact, many aren't comfortable with being called "leader" and would not describe themselves in that manner. However, what they do is to follow their passion for solving complex problems which, by definition, implies creativity and that they want to do this in the context of a team. What Ancona and Gregersen observed was that individuals definitely take on behaviors that would be clearly identified as "leading" but this behavior shifted depending on the task and who has the specific expertise. There was not a single individual identified as "the leader" but rather leadership appeared in an individual when they had a specific contribution to make and then passed on to another person once that contribution had been made.

I believe you seldom start a project without understanding how what you are making will matter to the user (the experience). Then how it would work (function) and then how it should look (its form).

Q: How does this impact the education system?
It is an interesting phenomenon that some of the best business schools are integrating design into their curriculum, and some of the best design schools are incorporating business education into their design programs. I was recently involved in a competition for entrepreneurs where many individuals were engaged to create new ideas for possible incubators.

As judges, we were able to see how teams naturally gravitated to people who had similar skill sets and ones that drifted together because of complimentary skill sets. The interesting thing was, those who were of similar backgrounds, be it engineering or design, came together first because they shared points of view. Those remaining, who offered different perspectives worked harder at understanding each other, but each contributed different points. It was a messy process, but out of that process came the winning entries. None of the winning designs came from teams that were concentrated with either all designers or all engineers. All of the winners were from organizations with diverse perspectives and capabilities—small, smart, and nimble **teams.**

Teams. The MIT team placed 1st among American universities in Elon Musk's 2019 SpaceX Hyperloop Pod Competition. Two of the significant reasons why this team won the challenge is because of a) the diversity of individuals involved and b) the fact that leadership emerged as the team worked together, and did not reside with any single individual. In this regard the book *Collective Genius* by Linda Hill, et.al. clearly shows how innovation depends on the leader being able to harvest the "collective genius" of all the people in the organization.

Similarly, the book *X-Teams* by Ancona and Bresman provides substantial research supporting the conclusion that small teams that are composed of a variety of perspectives are more creative and effective in achieving specific tasks. This is consistent with the "Wisdom of Teams" by Smith and Katzenbach, which also points out the advantage of diversity in decision making.

Q: At a recent university commencement, you began with the comment that "You don't know what you don't know." Can you elaborate on that?

When we celebrate graduations, we celebrate the enormous effort that has been put into accomplishing something, and the objective was so clear and significant we tend to feel we are now safe, accomplished, or complete. Those moments are times we remember and are essential in our lives as critical thresholds to change. The leadership and faculty have crafted a deliberate and intentional path for students to explore and to help build a future. This education is imbued with the knowledge of those with experience, talent, and skill who have preceded you. It is almost tribal in that what you have gone through what others both in your time and before you have also gone through. With this as the context, I was there to remind the graduates of a simple thing to help launch them into their respective careers. You don't know what you don't know. At this point, I'm sure they were thinking," I've worked so hard with some of the best minds available, all dedicated to giving me the tools needed togo out and seek my future." They think that not knowing what you don't know is a negative thing, somehow a failure of the system. In fact, it's a gift.

As a designer, I believe students today are graduating into one of the greatest possible careers, with an amazing legacy of changing things, inventing, creating, transforming their life, but—more importantly—transforming the lives of others. The creative endeavor is one of the few careers that can't be replaced simply by artificial intelligence. It is what fundamentally makes us human—to feel and imagine.

As a creative professionals we will never stop being curious. Regardless of how talented you are—or think you are—today, you will get better. You are on a lifelong journey to learn. You will discover what you don't know because you are in a field of change. The lessons you learn as a creative individual means you will never stop experimenting; always questioning why and always asking if there is a better way. If you are lucky enough, you will also get to do things that will define human progress.

Always rely on the skills you have been given. Believe in yourself. Trust your instinct and have the courage to follow your intuition. Experiment, fail, and try again. Focus on creating things that matter, not money. That will come. This idea is important as designers move forward in their careers. It is a way to remember to remain humble. To always question and critique. Create things that change human outcomes. Have no fear to change things for the better.

Q: How do you find the right people?
I don't think they are found. We believe in growth and development.I'm not sure who said this but I like the quote: "We are just people. On any given day we can be equally stupid, brilliant, confused, wonderful, disgusting or mad. Get over yourself." Personally I don't believe in arrogance, especially in any creative field. It is naive to me. Confidence is different to arrogance and is often confused. Anyone who I have known who was incredibly successful in a creative endeavor possessed an inherent humility and sensitivity. **The ones who believe they are genius never are**, and those who are, often are guilty of momentary brilliance and periods of self doubt.

The ones who believe they are genius never are. As Tim mentions, diversity in all of these forms help to create the space where innovation and creativity can emerge. Our experience is that when we bring a group of people together, say for instance an executive team that is struggling with a "wicked problem", instead of asking them to problem solve, we ask them to spend a week musing about what comes to mind as they go through their day with this "wicked problem" in the background. We then bring them together to share their associative thoughts. It is amazing the insight, depth of understanding and creative perspectives that emerge as a result of this process. Diversity is indeed significant and important. In fact, it is necessary, but without the structure, time and opportunity to harness that creativity, more often than not, it becomes a lost opportunity. Of course critical to creating that opportunity for diversity of thought and perspective to emerge, i.e. creativity, there has to be a fundamental sense of psychological safety within the team. Hal Gregersen's book *Questions Are the Answer* provides a very effective approach for focusing on questions rather than answers through the "Question Burst" methodology.

The creative process can and should sometimes be both wonderful and humiliating; incredibly satisfying and extraordinarily challenging. You will encounter all of this if you are successful.

Q: How would you describe the characteristics for a designer at Eight Inc.?
In the process of becoming incredibly skilled, but with the capacity and desire for greater understanding and growth on an emotional intelligence level. With a desire for fulfillment and growth from an individual ambition to a collective one. A thoughtful individual full of curiosity, whose interest must be fundamental but thoughtful. Secondly, to be humble; great designers do not think they are great. They understand it is an ongoing dialogue. Ian McKellen says he has played King Lear hundreds of times. He looks back on it each time knowing it could be better and enjoys the process of developing his craft. A designer must be capable of empathy, to be able to see yourself in the users point of view and to consider broad issues and impact.

Q: I can see where you find people who have deep understanding, but how do you filter for that broader kind of sensibility?
If you look at many of the people that we have in the company, we've structured it in such a way that we really look for people are more outliers to a traditional path in a design discipline. We may have an architect who comes from a particular education in architecture, but we tend to look at what are their other interests are. What are the other things that they may be doing. We've had an architect who was also a mountain bike racer, and he does other things like making custom design cycling components. The tendency is to look at people who probably don't fit into the standard way of doing things. They tend either to find a company where it's a typical kind of lifestyle, to find a nice fit, or join us where it's more of a different culture; one that allows that difference to be elevated.

We try to create an environment that attracts people. For people with a strength. Working from a strength leads to success and often to happiness. People with strong emotional intelligence. When you focus on those things, you do get the productivity and types of business outcomes you're looking for, but you get them by doing things that stimulate the most enjoyment and well-being for the person. Recent research from the University of Warwick showed that happiness made test subjects 12 percent more productive.

The question for designers is what fundamentally makes them happy. Ultimately we believe it's the work. Designers have a desire to grow and develop their skills. Older designers want to be part of a body of great work. This means the "happiness" factor in creative groups stems from the work and recognition they receive from the work. It's similar to applause for a stage actor. Recognition is a necessary part of the successful management of a creative team.

Q: It seems few companies have strength in dealing with creative teams?
It's not easy. It's not linear, and it engages emotions not everyone is comfortable dealing with. Because most people tend to operate on a functional level, they set functional objectives. Ideally, it's important to set the right creative development goals while ensuring that the practice is still feasible or possible. Experience plays a role, but so can other factors such as a culture that affects the ability to define successful outcomes, including socioeconomic background or geographic location. The type of industry will also be a factor.

It is essential to understand the principles of happiness and well-being, which people from all generations and backgrounds are seeking, but often creative endeavors can be challenging and have a negative impact on both happiness and prosperity. We look to augment those challenges with other aspects of our culture. With expressions of its brand value. It is vital for Eight Inc. or any company to express the values you believe in and to enable as best you can the well-being of employees. Ideally, you want to develop and retain the people that contribute to the work you are respected for. You will have a better chance of both finding and retaining the right people as well as connecting with your business relationships on a deeper level.

Q: How was your working relationship with Steve Jobs?
As with some people it was both personal and professional. Probably one of my favorite quotes about Steve is "he will be regarded as the person who unlocked the creativity of a whole generation." When we began, as he did with many people, he pushed us very hard. That was simply a durability and value test. To see that you had something to

contribute to the process, with knowledge or perspective, but also to be sure you were there because it was important to you. To see that you had something to contribute but to be sure you were there because it was important to you. There seemed to always be a **testing or qualification phase** to his key partners or working relationships.

Testing or qualification phase. One can imagine that behind this testing or qualification phase that Steve imposed on his partners and the working relationships there was a wish to challenge in order to be assured that there was indeed significant alignment in terms of the shared values. Because of his extreme focus on the relationship with customers, it makes sense that he would need to have that same connection with those key partners and working relationships. This links very clearly to the importance of trust which Tim mentions below.

We loved working with Steve because there was really no one to that point we had worked with who could push you and have remarkable critical thought to ensure the end design was right. Proposing design solutions is not hard. Doing it well is remarkably hard. When we began working with Steve, the company was very different to what it is today. The value and the number of people involved has changed dramatically. I think as one of two of the core agencies engaged at Apple for so long, we were able to see a remarkable transformation in Steve as well as the company.

Q: In what ways was he different?
When Steve Jobs would review work I seemed to see **two modes** that his thought process would take.

Two modes. It is clear from Tim's description of Steve that he possessed the capacity that, Dyer, Gregersen & Christensen (Innovator's DNA, 2011) found to be common in many of the CEOs of the top innovative companies: that these leaders had the capacity to function in both the discovery and delivery mode and were able to switch from one to the other. They could think and contribute in both domains while valuing the unique contribution of each. Depending on what was required in the process, they were able to appreciate the value of the rational and logical as well as of the creative and intuitive perspectives.

In many cases his feedback centered around the rational or logic dimension of the idea. You could almost see him running through a logic tree to evaluate if the design had merit. On the other hand he would just as easily approach the proposal on an intuitive level. What did it make him feel. The greatest work possessed a resolved logic portion, as many designs that followed did, but the real magic was when the design made you feel something. That it mattered to you in a way beyond what you expected. He was difficult to work with at times for many people because he was equally comfortable from both logic and intuitive ways of understanding things and few other people would be comfortable in both modes of critical thinking.

Q: There must be many learnings from the years working with Steve Jobs. What are some that influence great design?
In those 12 years we experienced many conditions that informs what is described as important design. Great design makes you ask questions. From high level to granular things. What do we stand for? What do we believe? Why should anyone care? What will we do? We are different because...We want to be remembered for...We love...don't love...We look... We act...We speak...How are we...Experienced, Relevant, Different, Perform. What do we feel?

Many of these types of considerations you find in people and companies with an honest ability for self evaluation and criticism. To do this through a process requires and sort of emotional intelligence. There is more to a company than its identity. The old branding agency model struggles because the conversation has moved on. A clear understanding of the simple parts of the distinctive experience is essential. What you do. What you stand for and how you engage in a relationship with our customers is at the heart of most great brands and great companies.

Q: It's clear you see design in a different way than most of us. Almost as a religion. Some part practice and some part belief or psychology.
Design matters. I don't believe it is a trivial pursuit. It is not well understood but it is a huge factor in how we exist. How we co-exist. Loyalty and preference come from a combination of being an incredible solution for things people need and an incredible design that allows people to engage with it. In our experience, the incredible people we work for and work with points to one truth. People who create great design, things that matter, have become engrained in our culture and our imagination. It is the understanding of the value of the experience with them. Things that people love. So where are we in the progression of design understanding and respect at the C-levels of companies or governments?

Maybe we need to be making things that matter to people matters more than ever.

Q: Leading growth and change in companies is likely one of the most difficult challenges business goes through. How would you approach this?
Sharing the solutions. Singapore stands as an example for many nations in crafting a livable city but with the objective of a more lovable one. Sharing those ideas around the globe and building a culture where diverse people share equal opportunity that combines their best interest with the best interests of the nation. Singapore has contributed to an approach of continuous learning and dialogue. Many countries could do well to learn from the Singapore experience. While the world is in constant change, the approach to solving difficult problems can be the key to success. The solutions that have produced the Singapore of today are not the same for the challenges of tomorrow. Ultimately to me, it is the design qualities that Lee Kuan Yew has provided for the next generation that may be his greatest legacy. These qualities will allow future generations of Singaporeans to face the next fifty years with the same intelligence, dignity, and grace.

Q: Results matter. What is the most important aspect you can identify with great results in your work?
Trust. I think we have been successful there because people put trust in our results and our approach. It fundamentally resonates with leaders. The most interesting thing about the work with any of our clients is getting to a point where there is a respect in the relationship and knowledge that they could rely on the work stretching the thinking.

Q: How do you work with those unable to deal with the unstructured side of a design process?
Design connections tend to come from non-linear paths and logical progressions. Those trained in linear thinking though will struggle the most with uncertainty. The leadership of the business must realize the challenges of the human side of disruption in the business. We had a client who was trained as an engineer and was a very structured thinker. He was able to take complex processes and large teams with independently

moving parts and drive them through a formal process to great success. His most challenging time was being in creative sessions where non-linear thought processes were occurring. He told us he couldn't be in the same room because the thought process was so disturbing to him.

The relationship must be an open and transparent engagement. There needs to be a precise definition and clarity around the process that recognizes where a pivot or shift can occur if new considerations are created. ***Definition + clarity*** that comes from intuition and experience and may not be part of a linear way of thinking. There must be a psychological safety for the exploration of new things. The only way to make new things is to approach things from a new direction. There has to be this fundamental trust in the process and goals of the project. The necessary tools of a creative culture are learning and development.

Q: Is this something business typically understands?
It varies. One of the best programs I am aware of is one where a business school (INSEAD) in this case and one of the worlds best design schools (Art Center College of Design) are operating an education rich exchange program to infuse business thinking into design and designers into a business context. The leading business schools such as INSEAD, Harvard and Rotman are taking the design world far more seriously than any other time in history.

Q: Is it easier for businesses who will struggle with creative teams to simply do nothing?
How do you quantify the risk of doing nothing? The business tendency is to rely on a less risky linear process (read "easier to understand and control") versus effectively managing an inherently inefficient, non-linear process. Virtually all business categories are under pressure from new technology adopters or startups. Even the most conservative industries are being challenged. In financial services, fintechs are putting pressure on traditional banks to improve quality of service, improve ease of use and improve loyalty and advocacy. The startups are more nimble and faster but traditional banks can compete if they move from the business-as-usual method to one focused on the customer experience versus the conventional internal view.

For Singapore, some of these things were not initially apparent but of great importance nonetheless. Since its inception, PM Lee had directed thousands of trees per year be planted across the country to ensure a truly livable city. As with all true design leaders, PM Lee Kuan Yew would not only know when a solution was correct, but he could also feel when it was not.

Q: Is the old method of procurement of design services dead?
Many leading American companies are struggling to keep up in the Apple era and the emerging designed economy. The procurement process is part of the problem. The idea that you can purchase creative services in the same way that you buy parts and equipment is as outdated as the industrial era.

The acquisition of creative teams through a scorecard procurement service demonstrates a lack of knowledge of creative team building and is a detrimental to successful competition today. It is merely another example of a legacy system that is being disrupted. Many companies are shifting to in-house creative teams or engaging creative consulting partners in long-term relationships as a way to create a compelling brand experience. This relationship is one of the most powerful tools businesses have, and probably the least understood. The depth of knowledge required to deliver strategic design successfully is not something you can achieve in the old model. The best and brightest creative talent does not work in the old procurement method any longer. The most talented will no longer work in an environment where the value of design is treated as a commodity, and its true business value is not fully understood. The lack of knowledge of the value of design is at the heart of the problem.

When a design is only understood as "look and feel" it typically reduces the selection process to a beauty contest. "Competitions" shopping for ideas will just ensure you see and attract C-level talent. It is more like creating an extraordinary team. Who has the skill and experience. The greatest teams want to have the greatest athletes in the game who can work well together.

Apple and other leading companies are gaining a competitive advantage by building creative teams into the organization. The **success** comes from assigning experienced leaders of design talent and fostering an environment that attracts and retains the most brilliant designers. In the survival of the fittest, great companies will better understand the creative component and the others will become weaker.

Success. I think the point here that Tim is making is that design, that is to say, creativity and innovation, need to be built into the DNA of the organization so that every function, every division and every team has a yearly creative, innovation challenge that they are required to fulfill. I recall visiting the innovation center at PayPal in which they were showcasing the marketplace of the future and one of the requirements within PayPal was that literally every team in the organization (e.g. finance marketing, procurement and even the innovation team) had to have and innovation goal every year as part of their yearly goal setting process.

Q: You identified some qualities for success. What would you point to for others to consider?

Develop a Design IQ: Great design creates value. Companies need to identify a creative and successful design team engagement. It means changing the market compensation model. Many design-led companies pay more than the market for their creative team leadership to attract and retain the best. It is difficult for traditional consultancies to compete. The problem with outright acquisitions is the relationship to the design sector of the business compared to the typical. Fundamentally design-led businesses must prove their value and when they do the old pay-per-haircut model of engaging creative teams is likely to change.

Drop Zone, Dubai, 2014

Beware of Best Practices

Most companies look at their peers as examples of what to do. We look at your peers for what not to do. You seldom hear this from consultants.

Drop Zone, Dubai, 2014

Drop Zone, Dubai, 2014

Drop Zone, Dubai, 2014

TOW-AWAY
NO STOPPING

Union Larder, San Francisco, 2014

LARDER
OYSTERS
Fanny Bay -B.C.
Walker Creek
Beau Soleil -NB.
Marin Miyagi -CA.
CHARCUTERIE
Coppa
Toscano
Mortadella
Bresaola
Varzi
Sopressata
Prosciutto
Lonza
Speck
Saussison Sec
Jamón Ibérico

Union Larder, San Francisco, 2014

Oslo National Museum of Art, Oslo, 2009

Oslo National Museum of Art, Oslo, 2009

Oslo National Museum of Art, Oslo, 2009

Oslo National Museum of Art, Oslo, 2009

Bently Heritage Distillery, Minden, 2019

Bently Heritage Distillery, Minden, 2019

Lissa Flatware, Dansk, 1994

Q: What do you mean when you say beware of best practices? Emulating a peer or competitor for operational efficiency is a common business practice. Emulating your competitor when defining your customer experience is very dangerous. Emulation leads to parity, and parity in a category leads to commodity. The best way to commoditize your business is to follow your competitors. The best way to make your competitor a leader is to become a follower.

Originality creates value. Human experience is stronger when it is differentiated and connecting to people on an emotional level versus a rational one. Best practices tend to commoditize everyone and everything in the category.

A reliance on best practices is fundamentally a backward-looking proposition. It relies on existing practices to learn from or emulate. The problem is, it does not take into account the potential of new solutions and new conditions. What does this tell us? It could be that companies struggle to create significantly differentiated products but what I see more frequently is that, when business resorts to best practices to deliver those products, they tend to emulate each other and reduce the fundamental value of their offerings. This can easily become a crutch, and it's the problem with research as a solution to competitive challenges for business. This is where creativity has an incredible competitive advantage.

Best practices. I am reminded of the phrase, "the answer murders the question" in that it seems to me that best practices represent the answer to a question. This results in most people no longer thinking. As a consequence new ideas and creativity drop, if not completely disappear, and the original question that was asked has been forgotten. Understanding social defenses enables the leader to address this "mind stopping" dynamic. Often the rush to adopt "best practice" is based on the anxiety of "what to do" and the need to come to a quick solution. In such a situation, "best practice" is applied in order to reduce the anxiety caused by uncertainty. The consequence is often that the best practice is suboptimal or in fact even destroying value. "Best practice" can be seen as the "crutch" which is a social defense. While a crutch might, in special circumstances, be essential, the risk is that it becomes a way to avoid the difficult questions, which makes it a social defense. Rather than being an aid temporarily, employed in order to achieve a larger goal, it enables the executive team to avoid their anxiety in terms of "what to do?" by following best practices. In this sense, "best practice" murders the questions and kills the creativity. Hal Gregersen's book "*Questions are the Answers*" offers another approach to addressing the rush to "best practice" by encouraging leaders to ask more questions and to avoid the temptation to find quick answers, which is often the basis for defaulting to "best practice".

Q: So best practices are not a solution for businesses that want to compete?
For business operations it is fine. For differentiation it's a disaster. It's fine, when you're entering a category, to understand what your competitors are doing in that category. But to emulate what they do from the end-user experience perspective can limit the potential of that business. Many companies become noticed by offering the same thing in the same way. The competitive difference is often a lower-cost value proposition. In many ways it's easier to look at reducing costs when entering the market, but it misses the opportunity for new potential that could make the company extraordinary.

It can be extremely difficult to get people to think beyond this frame of reference. In our experience, companies that emulate their competitors erode their differentiation value and therefore weaken their competitive posture in a market.

Q: Businesses seem to be expressing a renewed interest in design. What do you think is driving this?
Competition. Competitive threats come in many forms, and the ability to adapt and change is fundamentally at the heart of survival. It's been the case for virtually every species, and the same is true in business.

Adaptation and change are often the most difficult things we do as individuals and evolving organizations, because of existing structures and functioning models that increase difficulty. What is interesting is to see companies who are struggling to keep up with their increased rate of change begin to understand and recognize the value of strategic design. In fact, the rate of change is raising those people best equipped to deal with change, and they are likely strategic designers.

Design by definition is about change. In a volatile, transformative environment, creativity can bring enormous value if the company knows how to work with creative teams. The most competitive companies possess a high-performance creative team as an integral part of their business.

Q: What are examples of brands in both China and the US with different differentiation perspectives?
In China, the technology sector is interesting because of the cult-like following of companies like Xiaomi who were built around an idea. This is how these companies are competing with the bigger and more deeply capitalized companies such as Huawei.

Huawei has been making technology in China for many years across a lot of sectors but only recently has started to build its brand in a way that people can connect with. It is technically very strong, well capitalized and government aligned. In fact, it is common to see companies that come from a manufacturing background struggle with the transition to a compelling brand. Companies like Xiaomi have an advantage because they were built around what the company can do for people versus what type of technology they can produce.

They tend to discount the smaller businesses because of their size of capital, in much the same way as Dell and Nokia dismissed the smaller competitors (Apple at that time) in their categories. The challenge is not only with new or emerging companies but especially those that are older with more legacy resistance in their organizations. Samsung has always had an internal struggle determining if it's a brand or a manufacturer. It prides itself on the ability of its manufacturing systems to turn on a dime if the next new product in demand happens to change. It's primary competitive advantage emulates others faster and at a lower price than most. The risk, of course, is commoditization.

Q: What are successful examples of Design Leadership?
Most think of successful large-scale companies, but design leadership can also apply to governments and other types of organizations. Singapore is a world-class city-state nation, a major commercial hub, and a financial center. It is the envy of many other nations. Accolades for Singapore's accomplishments have come from leaders the world over. Many countries large and small look at Singapore for best practices and new ideas. But I believe Singapore is also a designed success. Singapore, at 50+ years old, has proven to rise above virtually every challenge with a remarkable and distinct approach. From conception,

through execution, almost every aspect of the country seems to have been created through a considered and disciplined process, designed specifically for the greater good of the people and in the best interest of the country. Singapore could not achieve the success without design leadership and key design traits heralded by the first Prime Minister of Singapore, Mr. Lee Kuan Yew.

To me, great leaders design with positive human outcomes in mind. Designing for companies like Apple, Virgin, and many other business innovators, we have seen how design can change the way people think, feel, and do things; how design can transform peoples lives in incredibly powerful ways. When I think of true masters of design leadership, I have to put former Singaporean PM. Lee Kuan Yew near the top of this list.

Q: So governments can benefit from creative process?
Innovation is when people adopt a vision that it is able to transform people's lives for the better. Lee Kuan Yew, most commonly understood as the political leader and one of the founding fathers of Singapore, demonstrated what seems to reflect some of the best aspects of a good design process: a creative approach to problems, originality, empathy, focus, and passion. It is the delivery of great vision that will transform challenges into a new reality. Design thinking is a start, but only design can deliver real transformation. The same qualities that make leading companies among the best in the world in business have been vital to creating a prosperous Singapore nation.

Q: What was specific to his brand of leadership?
Qualities of design. Many of Singapore's successes have been well documented, but I would instead think about Singapore from the perspective of creating a great nation through design and innovation. Our experience designing with Steve Jobs was incredible. It provided insights into the way this remarkable man thought about everything he created: how to approach design; how to lead; and how to build success. His focus through the act of design and making—whether hardware, software, or retail—was on things that would matter to people: a shift from Return on Investment thinking to Return on Experience. With Lee Kuan Yew I saw many of the same qualities I experienced with Steve. Lee Kuan Yew

delivered on an incredibly challenging scale as he dealt with issues concerning the ups and downs of a nation, redefinition of the economy and the transformation of a society; things that affected the lives of millions of people.

Great design leaders deal with complex issues. They can find solutions that offer the best possible fit with the context that surrounds it, creating experience that connects people to their activities and the environment that surrounds them. Since the founding of Singapore, the challenges for this small Southeast Asian country have been significant. From protecting itself against local and international threats, to understanding the subtlety and nuance necessary to create a home for a mix of peoples with diverse cultural and ethnic backgrounds, Singapore may well be the most diverse nation on Earth with the lowest incidence of crime and racial conflict.

Q: So leaders of all forms need to embrace creativity in order to be successful?
Leadership by design must deal with both **rational and emotional outcomes.**

Rational and emotional outcomes. The point here is that the rational aspect applies to our intellectual understanding whereas the emotional component is much more about the heart and the feelings and emotions that resonate deep within us as we experience the design (*Thinking, Fast and Slow* by Daniel Kahneman, 2011). When both the intellectual or rational as well as the emotional resonate together within us there is a connection between the head and the heart that takes place and leads us to commitment, engagement and a sense of belonging.

In the political sense this is always the case, but in types of leadership it is essential to look at two kinds of outcomes. It is a unique ability to see things through both rational and emotional thought processes. This sensitivity has led to not only successful business objectives but also the quality of life outcomes.

This leadership comes from the ability to see and value context—essential for people and activities to add to a larger whole and for conditions of success. For Singapore, some of these things were not initially apparent. The design of this nation has been understood to be both economically viable, remarkably livable but also factors that make it a lovable place to live. One example is that since its inception, PM Lee planted thousands of trees per year across the country to ensure a truly livable city. As with all true design leaders, PM Lee Kuan Yew would not only know when a solution was correct but he could also feel when it was not.

Q: You identified some qualities for success. What would you point to for others to consider?
Focus. Focused execution of an idea is essential to delivering the vision. Great design is about building interdependent practices and partnerships. It was a key for Apple. Singapore has built an increasingly stronger national fabric by connecting meaningful conversations with those who possess in-depth knowledge of methods and capabilities. The focus continues to be on making a more significant outcomes for its citizens. It has a strong middle class, while the generation of pioneers who helped develop the country have been honored and respected by those who have been given a nation of progress and wealth.

Excellence and rigor. Performance matters. An emphasis on excellence and rigor has created prosperity, safety, education and excellent health care. One in six households in Singapore possess more than SG $1m in wealth. While income inequalities still exist, the trend is positive with growth and the value of being admired by many nations.

Collaboration. Great design leaders collaborate with great people, build diverse teams, and include the full range of different communities and disciplines. They recognize this as the basis for a healthy ecosystem. They build teams that cover a variety of skilled individuals who reflect a similar desire for the greatest good and are dedicated to the vision of the leader. Singapore builds leadership that resists the attraction to the corruption that neighboring nations have been unable to uproot, by paying equal to or better than current salaries of similar positions in the private sector. Leaders are drafted with a balance of wisdom from the experienced industry, and new leaders with youthful energy are elevated from across the nation.

Sharing the solutions. Singapore stands as an example for many nations in crafting solutions for creating a living city. In sharing those ideas around the globe and building a culture where diverse people share equal opportunity that combines their best interest with the best interests of the nation, Singapore has contributed to an approach of continuous learning and dialogue.

Q: Should other countries look at this approach as a model?
Many countries could do well to learn from the Singapore experience. While the world is in constant change, the approach to solving difficult problems can be the key to success. A company or a nation who consist of a design-aware population has an incredible competitive advantage. The solutions that have produced the Singapore of today are not the same for the challenges of tomorrow. Ultimately, it is the design qualities that Lee Kuan Yew has provided for the next generation that may be his greatest legacy. These qualities will allow future generations to face the next 50 years with the same intelligence, dignity, and grace.

Q: So if you summarize Return on Experience how would you describe how it fits in the business world?
Companies compete to create value. Business success is dependent on value creation. Value creation is a function of creating successful experience that people adopt. Successful human outcomes. Great experience is things that matter to people delivered in ways that matter to people. To compete, companies must understand their relationship to people in ways that allow them to maximize their potential. Companies that successfully deliver this create a competitive advantage. For us this creates Return on Experience.

Q: When you look at the body of work and the impact you are having, what continues to drive you?
We have the opportunity to be part of the conversation. We're just trying to leave something behind.

Eight Inc., San Francisco, 2011

Acknowledgments

I want to credit and thank those who have been a critical part of the Eight Inc. community. Each has contributed creativity, thought, and talent, and has had a deep influence on and as a part of Eight Inc. Each of these people have helped to progress design just a bit more. It is to these amazing individuals and their families that this book is dedicated.

Vasco Agnoli, Kambiz Ahmadi, Sherief Ahmed, Alexandra Almaral, Amelia Altavena, Luke Altenau, Erik Anderson, Katherine Apfelstadt, Angel Araujo, Ini Archibong, Jonathan Arena, Mateo Atti, Andrew Au, Philip Bailey, Sheldon Baker, Chino Balagtas, Paami Barnett, Nic Bauer, Alex Bautista, Leonie Beck, Hermann Behrens, Pete Bell, Karina Benloucif, David Benton, Alan Best, Hitasha Bhatia, Selenne Bishop, Nikolai Blackie, Neshemah Blackwell, Dave Blendis, Carrie Bobo, Nuri Boler, Julian Boxenbaum, Teresa Boydon, Kristen Braasch, Richard Brace, Alex Bradley, Robert Bradsby, Jon Bruni, Emily Brooks, William Bryant, Jade Burns, Noah Campeau, Teresa Campos, Brett Cattani, Rebecca Caution, Jacqueline Cavalieri, Jane Cee, Ricardo Cepeda, Elliot Charles, Lisa Charron, Veronica Cheann, Eddison Chen, Cherry Chen, Linao Chen, Yun Haua Chen, Michelle Cheng, Olivier Chételat, Joanna Cheung, Peter Chew, Euna Chi, Vivien Chin, Grace Chou, Selig Chow, Jasmine Chung, Hilary Clark, Timothy Clark, Bryan Collins, Zhao Conglong, Brandon Cook, Laura-Louise Cottle, Patrick Cox, Brian Cutler, Philip Czapla, Scott Davis, Alexandra De Gedeon, Nick Der, Craig Dimond, Christopher Dobson, Ashley Dominguez, Wong Mei Yuen Dora, Wendy Dorrel, Lamine Drame, Siyao Du, Andrew Duffus, Loana Dumitrescu, Adam Eastburn, Alina Eberly, Joshua Echevarria, Christopher Egervary, Heiner Eibel, Michael Ely, Mary Emerson, Rein Estigoy, Julie Faris, Alessio Fasciolo, Casey Feeney, Reed Fehr, Marvin Fernandes, Robert Findlay, Eleanor Flanders, Ploipailin Flynn, Jiantong Gao, Alicia Garcia, Mat Giles, Daniel Gittleman, Luke Godward, Rhonda Goyke, Matt Goyke, Ingrid Graff-Cailleaud, Ziyi Guo, Shreya Gupta, Andre Ha, Pierre Habib, Emily Hake, Jethro Hale, Erin Haney, Nazma Haque, Kira Hassert, Bella Hayes, Celine Hayman, Hannah Hayman, Brandie Heinel, Andrew

Heirons, David Herman, Marc Hibos, Tamara Hill-Berndt, Gideon Hillman, Yuko Hiroi, Mathew Hollingsworth, Fred Holt, Melissa Hon, James Hood, Kristy Hsu, Po-Jui Huang, Aditya Hukama, Alex Hulme, David Hunter, Nick Hussain, Eugene Hwang, David Hwang, Rebecca Iguchi, Chie Ikeda, Bojana Ilievski, Neslihan Isik, Leyla Jalilie, Kimberli Jensen, Sandhya Jethnani, Helen Jewitt, Chum Jiaxin, Sarah Johnson, Jessica Judge, Matt Judge, Ryoji Karube, Julie Keiner, Leon Kerpel, Tiffany-Jade Kelly, Abdul Basit Khan, Kaidi Kikas, Roy Kim, Ji-In Kim, Louise King, Heather King, Peter Kirby, Julia Klotz, Caty Kobe, Leigh Anne Kobe, Jil Kobe, Madeline Kobe, Mathew Kobe, Jaroslaw Komuda, Erik Kramer, Daniel Krivens, Darko Krstevski, Edmond Kuan, Hans Ladegaard, Lea Lagasse, Anita Lai, Brent Lambert, Lisa Lamont, Georges Lane, Jeff Lashins, Andrew Lauck, Ruby Lawrence, Doo Ho Lee, Lauren Lee, Michelle Lee, Jane Lee, Stella Lee, Jon Levenson, Mengyu Li, Shirley Li, Celina Li, Min Liang, Evan Liao, Steve Lidbury, Conrad Lim, Chia-Ying Lin, Joseph Lin, Alan Lin, Wong Wan Ling, Michael Lisboa, Samuel Lising, Mark Little, Gideon Littman, Kaidi Liu, Russell Lloyd, Ashleigh Louison, Sara Lu, Betty Lui, Yan Ma, Euan MacLennan, Daniela Madina-Mate, Jed Maiden, Andrea Mairui, Ashlee Major-Moss, Kirk Malanchuk, Alexander Maly, Mark Mancuso, Stacey Mar, Karen Mar, Martie Martinez, Robert Mathewson, Charlie McBride, Rob McIntosh, Matthew McNerney, Cecilia Mei, David Meisenzhal, Richa Menke, Audrey Miller, Samuel Miller, Gordon Millichap, Hector Moll-Carrillo, Jose Monteiro, Alison More, Jacob More, Stacie Morrow, Frankie Morton, Colleen Mote, James Mulligan, Shivangi Narke, Steven Nebel, Kerstin Neurohr, Ian Nicholson, Amanda Nielson, Joe Nobles, Markus Nonn, Wilhelm Oehl, Mandy Oeni, Sunny Oh, Manuel Oh, Sun Duck Oh, Scott Oliver, Derrick Ong, Katherine Ong, Doreen Ong, Jared Otake, Mihoko Ouchi, David Owen, William Paluch, Jaxe Pan, Stella Papadopoulos, Soo Youn Park, Dylan Parry, Niels Paulus, Emily Pavling, Gavin Pearce, Kerry Penalver, Jasmine Peterhans, Joshua Philippe, Vinh Pho, Paolo Poliedri, Tudor Prisacariu, Henry Proudlove, Isabella Purvis, Rob Pybus, Laura Pye, Julien Queyrane, Olaf Quoohs, Alan Ramsey, Francis Real, Sean Rees, Joseph Reihl, Anna Relova, Anna Richell, Kristin Ring, Andrea Rocha, Jamie Rogers,

Gretchen Romano, Louise Rowley, Daniel Sabat, Shabbar Sagarwala, Asha Saiyd, Adam Sakia, Evelyn Troden Santiago, Evelina Sausina, Claudia Schaller, Mario Schellingerhout, Christine Schneider, George Schon, Eric Scott, Ang Teck Seng, Jean A. Servaas, Mayumi Seto, Troy Shelton, Vera Shur, Jonathan P. Siegel, Emily Silet, Scott Smardo, Francis Smith, Calvin Soh, Sung Bae Son, Rupinder Sond, Fran Soper, Dan Sowten, Janice Stainton, Davis Stams, Cara Starke, Zoe Stavrou, Craig Stewart, Jeff Strasser, William Strobel, Brian Studak, George Such, Alexandra Suffield, Nicole Sun, Mahadevan Supaya, Dominic Symons, Laura Szu-Tu, Iso Takesawa, Cherie Tallett, Mikki Tam, William Tammen, Alexander Tan, Kelly Tan, Ayako Tanaka, Olivia Tang, Jintana Tantinirundr, Daniel Chong Joh Tar, Ryan Tate, Lucinda Tay, Kong Yee Teng, Massimiliano Terio, Simon Thai, Lam Sook Theng, Antonieta Trabassas, Gabriel Trujilo, Miwa Tsurusaki, Joanne Tucker, Melanie Turner, Enric Turull, Genry Umali, Patrick Edison Uy, Yana Vainshtok, Elyna Vijay, Dante Vinciguerra, Wolfgang Voegtli, Khuyen Vu, Allison Wachtel, Man Lai Wan, Prangmat Wanapinyosak, Luke Ward, George Waters, Alison Weill, Allison Weiner, Stephen Wells, Erik West, Jenny West, Dan Westwood, Sophie Widjaja, Harriet Williams, Brooke Williams, Roxanne Wilson, Yoana Wiman, Viviane Winkler, Angelo Wisco, Angela Wong, Stephanie Wong, Martin Woreczek, Serenay Yilmaz, Jie Siang Yong, Sarah Yoo, Cameron Youds, Chu Yuet, Kong Yuzhou, Jingxuan Zhang, Tracy Zhou, Qing Zhou, Yanjie Zhou, and Lisa Zhu.

And special thanks to Cherie, Lynn and Dylan who without their dedication this book would not have been possible.

Design is never done in a vacuum, thanks to the many significant contributors, clients, friends, and colleagues:

Mona Abadir-Applegate, Marwan Abedin, Teresa Abenoja, Rony Abovitz, Maurice Action, Yuki Adachi, Steph Adams, Bruce "Albi" Albinson, Sandra Soto Alfaro, Olga Alter, Neil Ambler, Sig Anderson, Jake Anderson, Anthony Ang, Chris Angerame, Sydney Applegate, Thomas Applegate, Eijii Araki, Edwin Archy, Robert Arko, Aloysius Arlando, Jennifer Armstrong, Hiroki Asai, Andrew Ashman, Susan Avarde, Darren Baird, Richard Baker, Federico Barbieri, Bill Barnett, Kit Baron, Michael Barry, Dr. Swan Gin Beh, Yves Behar, Christopher Bently, Charles Best, Hakan Binbasgil, Wic Bhanubandh, Dinesh Bhatia, Dave Billmaier, Abdulla Mohammed Bin Habtoor, Katie Bisbee, Brad Bissell, Sylvia Bistrong, Peter Bithos, David Black, George Blankenship, Jerry Blanton, Bob Bobbera, Cesar Bocanegra, Nikolai Bogdanovic, Jeremy Bogen, Alessandro Bogliolo, Peter Bohlin, Nikolai Bojic, Moti Booskila, Robert D. Booth, Bob Borchers, Jeremy Borden, Peter Borer, Michael Borosky, Debbi Boughtflower, Doug Boyd, Stephen Brady, Tyler Brager, Sir Richard Branson, Mark Breitenberg, Chris Briers, Tim Brown, Lucas Bruggermann, Dena Brumpton, Bob Brunner, Christian D Bruun, Dr. Lorne Buchman, Darrin Buckley, Chalaluck Bunnag, Bruce Burdick, Anne Burdick, Busy Burr, Pascal Cagni, Lyn Calim, Joe Caliro, Susanne Calkins, Cory Lynn Calter, Greg Caputo, Olivier Carnohan, Olivia Carnohan, Jeremy Cavendish, Diana Cawley, Jeffrey Cha, Don Chadwick, Suanne Chan, Bill Chang, Bobby Change, Chakrit Chanrungsakul, Khaled Chatila, Tim Chen, Patrick Chia, Gary Chock, Joseph Chong,Yeo Piah Choo, Vinson Chua, David Claire, Lee Clow, David Comfort, Robert Comstock, Shawmut Design and Construction, Tim Cook, Dee Cooper, Karen Cooper, James Coppack, Panasonic Digital Communications Corporation, The Nomura Corporation, Paolo Dalla Corte, Justin Counts, Philip Course, Chris Cowert, Matthew Crabbe, Daisy Cresswell, Christopher Cribb, Cliff Crosbie, Ernest Cu, Emmanuel Daniel, Basil Darwish, Mike Dauberman, Julie David, Jeff David, Robert

C. Davidson Jr., Professor Gavin Davis, David Day, Mariana Zobel de Ayala, Viran De Silva, Roel de Vries, Bill Delaney, Daniel DeLong, Markus Diebel, Suzan Sabanci Dincer, Sean Divine, Jeff Doan, Sue Doell, Tom Dolan, PJ Doland, Casey Drake, Andy Dreyfus, Matthew Driver, Ge Drossaet, Ivan Dubovsky, Nicole Dummett, Tim Duncan, Will East, Gaylord Eckles, Landon Eckles, Andrea Koerselman Edmunds, Gary Edstein, Adam Edwards, Erich Christian Elkins, Kohei Eguchi, Darrelle Eng, John Ermatinger, Jay J. Esopenko, Fabio Fontainha, Brian Fairben, Marcus Fairs, Tan Family, Francis Farrow, Yogesh Farswani, Tabiatha Faust-Singer, John Felicetti, Ellie Fernandes, Michael Fernbacher, Joe Ferry, Ben Finane, Michael Fisher, Henning Flaig, Eugene Fluery, Stephen K.K. Fong, Fabio Fontainha, Nicholas Foo, Michael Foong, Rosanna Fores, Gerhard Fourie, Zac Fried, Rudolf Frieling, Dale Frost, Jackie Fugere, Omar Al Futtaim, John Gagnier, Philippe Galtié, David Garcia, Courtnie Gastinel, Herbert Gee, Ali Ghanbarian, Fadi Ghandour, Carlos Ghosn, Chaz Giles, Beh Swan Gin, Christoph Goebel, Gordon Goff, Brad Goodall, Srini Gopalan, Garrett Gourlay, Margaret Grade, Nancy Green, Tim Greenhalgh, Elliott Grimshaw, William T. Bill Gross, Harrison Grundy, Robbie Habib, Colleen Haesler, Abdallah Hageali, Saeed Mohammad Ali Mohammad Al Hajeri, Koichi Hara, Dennis Hardcastle, Martin Hargreaves, Amran Hassan, Bob Hasse, Karl Heizelman, Julian Hemming, Lee Seow Hiang, Hamaguchi Hideshi, Dan Hill, Elliot Hill, Kit Hinrichs, Adrian Hobt, Chris Holt, Debby Hopkins, Mark Hoplamazian, Skip Horner, Jerrard Hou, Andrew Hoyem, Hosain Hrahman, Stephen Hubner, Jean Hung, Caleb Hunt, Low Cheaw Hwei, Nacasa & Partners Inc., The staff of MS Partner Inc., Isometrix, Jonathan Ive, Jarrod Jablonski, Bassam Jabry, Anuj Jain, Alexander Jarvis, Ameer Jumabhoy, Amanda Jenkins, Antony Jenkins, Steven P. Jobs, Steve Jobs, Ron Johnson, Alice Jones, Lei Jun, Glenn Kaino, Kevin Kaiser, Ceren Kalkan, Max Kantelia, Joanna Kao, Joakim Karske, Christopher Kay, Yazaki Kazuhiko, Neil Kee, Laura Keenan, Shireen El Khatib, Roy Kim, Peter Kirby, Paul Klass, Fritha Knudsen, Yumi Kobayashi, Miyamoto Koichi, Susy Korb, Richard Koshalek,

Warren Krawchuk, Gregory Kraff, Reed Krakoff, Richard J. Kramer, Dick Kramlich, Pamela Kramlich, Richa Kung, Richard and Vicki Küng, Suhail Kurban, Kevin Kuroiwat, Agnes Kwek, Karen Kwek, Neeta Lachmandas, George Laine, Evon Lam, John and Tracy Lamond, Cathy Lapuz, Sara Larsen, Francesco Lagutaine, Jonathan Larson, Edwin Lee, Dale Lee, Chevlin Lee, Chan Fong Leng, Steve Leonard, Ryan Leslie, Victor Li, Cristina Lily, Augustine Lim, Yvonne Lim, Gabriel Lim, Jeremy Lim, Dinal Limbachia, James Linsley, Michael Lints, Stefan Liske, Leon Liu, Eva Liu, Chia Kee Lock, Karla Losen, Cheaw Hwei Low, Neal Luke, Peter Madden, Michael Maharam, Craig Makino, Dubai Crown Prince Sheikh Hamdan bin Mohammed bin Rashid Al Maktoum, Ellen Maloney, Theodora Mantzaris, Gerald Marion, Primo Mariotti, Helal Saeed Al Marri, Darren Marshall, Hiroshi Matsui, Jimbo Masahiko, Takaaki Matsumoto, Carl Coryell-Martin, Bruce Mau, Rebecca McCarty, Josh Mckay, Kevin McSpadden, Clark Melrose, Callistus Chong Teck Meng, Louis Minuto, Jeanie Mitsunaga, Karl Mohan, Sopnendu Mohanty, Marie Moore, Scott Morris, Miwa Murasaki, Prajna Murdaya, Glenn Murphy, Priyanka Nadkarni, Shiro Nakamura, Tan Chin Nam, Brad Nash, The Nautilus Hyosung Company, Harri Nieminen, Melody Nobis, Rie Nørregaard, Charlotte Nors, Dan and Sean Nowell, Kawin Nualkhair, Elizabeth Nyamayaro, James O'Callaghan, Chris O'Connor, Neil Heslop OBE, Ran Oehl, Deepak Ohri, Colin Okashimo, His Excellency Omar bin Sultan Al Olama, Simon Ong, Cheech Ong, Sasha Orloff, Yusaka Ota, Jong Fa Ou, Alex Ou, Elisa Ours, Ricardo Outi, Peter Overy, Arda Ozel, Chonpreya Pacharaswate, Joel Palix, KK Pan, Raul Parades, Jayesh Parekh, Dan Paris, Thomas Patterson, Raymond Pettitt, The Directors and Staff of the Phillip and Patricia J. Frost Museum of Science, Khoo Ee Ping, Aaron Pocock, Ruth Poh, Bernice Polifka, Tim Power, Tobias Puehse, Nauman Puyarji, Lindsay Pyne, Omar Qureishi, Amy Radin, Aruna Raghavan, Rakhi Rajani, Kimberly Rath, Heather Reisman, Andrew Rettig, Rise, Dan Riccio, Ed Roberts, Ted Root, John Rose, Glenn and

Susan Rothman, The RTC Corporation, Christine Ruffley, Dr. Amina Al Rustamani, Natalie Ryan, Makoto Sakaguchi, Mel Salgado, James B. Salter, Dilhan Pillay Sandrasegara, Marwan Al Sarkal, Marc Sasserath, Pauline Sato, Mark Schermers, Ingo Schweder, Norm Schwab, Diego Scotti, Mike Sears, Jeff Semenchuk, Deon Senturk, Gonul Serbest, Jim Seuss, Suresh Shankar, Marwan A. Shehadeh, Xavier Shield, Cindy Silverman, Vijay Sivaraman, Nathan Smith, Andy Smith, Jill Smith, Simon Smith, Travis Smith, Calvin Soh, Alki Sonitis, Lady Frances Sorrell, Sir John Sorrell, Manuel Sosa, Erik Spiekermann, Peter Spreenberg, Robert Stannard, Michael Stephenson, Frank Steslow, Judy Stokker, Claudio Storelli, Tom Suiter, Michael Sweeney, Dagmara Szulce, Takuya Takei, Anthony Tan, Christian Tan, Danny Tan, Kiat How Tan, Patrina Tan, Hooi Ling Tan, Ivan Tan, Joe Tan, Tharin Tan, Hans-Ulrich Tanner, Tim Tate, Manabu Tatekawa, Scarlet Taylor, Angelita Teo, Jeffrey Tham, Frank Thaler, Charlie Thompson, Alan Threadgold, Titiya Chooto, Susan Towers, Craig Trettau, Jeffrey Trott, Serdar Turan, Lee Turlington, Greg Turpan, Serkan Unal, Giovanni Viterale, Gopal Vittal, Ko Chee Wah, Andy Waldeck, Mark Wee, Holger Weltz, Steve Wilhite, Seve Wilhite, Kejuan Wilkins, Paul Wiste, Anissa Wong, The Management and Craftspeople of Fetzer Architectural Woodworking, Jun Hua Aaron Wong, Jeremy Wright, Winston Wright, Keith Yamashita, Kevin Yeaman, Jacks Yeo, Dr. Swee Choo Yeoh, Rachel Yeong, Maridol D. Ylanan, Atsuko Yoshitsugu, Anupam Yog, Janet Young, Ted Younkin, Scott Yu, Anna Zappettini, Huang Zijuan, Melissa Ziweslin, Kathy Xu 徐新, Du Guoying 杜国楹, Yang Haoyong 杨浩涌, Bin Lin 林斌, Bai Rubing 白如冰, James Zheng 郑捷, Jason Huang 黄峰.

Index

Image Credits

Cover & Back Cover, Globe Live, Manila, 2018. Photography by Nascasa & Partners.
10, 11, Apple Genius Bar, Bologna, 2011. Credit: Apple.
12, 13, Apple Store Fifth Avenue, New York, 2006. Credit: Apple.
14, Apple Store, London, 2006. Credit: Apple.
15, Apple Macworld, San Francisco, 2007. Credit: Apple.
16, 17, Apple Store Fifth Avenue, New York, 2006. Credit: Apple.
18–21, Nike Jordan Brand Carmelo Anthony Installation, New York, 2011. Photography by SGM Photography.
22, 23, Wolff Olins, New York, 2005. Credit: Wolff Olins.
26–28, Majid Al Futtaim, Wonderbar, Dubai, 2017. Image by Eight Inc. Singapore.
36, Newmeyers' States of Being Diagram.
38, Fair Process Diagram. Source: Ludo Van der Heyden, INSEAD.
46–51, Apple Watch Launch, Cupertino, 2014. Credit: Apple.
52–53, Apple MacWorld, San Francisco, 2009. Credit: Apple.
54–57, Apple MacWorld, San Francisco, 1999. Credit: Apple.
58, 59, Apple MacWorld, New York, 2000. Credit: Apple.
60, Apple Store, Palo Alto, 2001. Credit: Apple.
74–76, Shimano Cycling World, Singapore, 2014. Photography by Sparkling Eye Production Pte Ltd.
77–85, Shimano Cycling World, Singapore, 2014. Photography by Aaron Pocock.
80, 81, Virgin Atlantic Clubhouse, San Francisco, 2000. Photography by Tim Hursley.
82–85, Virgin Atlantic Airline A380, 2006. Sketches by Eight Inc.
86–89, Virgin Hotel and Casino, Las Vegas, 2006. Renderings by Eight Inc.
90–92, QUT App, Australia, 2016. Image by Eight Inc. Singapore.
106–109, Virgin Atlantic Clubhouse, San Francisco, 2000. Photography by Tim Hursley.
110, 111, Xiaomi Flagship Store, Shenzhen, 2018. Credit: Xiaomi.
112, 113, Xiaomi Flagship Store, Shenzhen, 2018. Sketches by Eight Inc.
114, 115, Xiaomi Flagship Store, Shenzhen, China, 2018. Renderings by Eight Inc.
116, 117, Xiaomi Flagship Store, Shenzhen, 2018. Credit: Xiaomi.
118, Xiaomi Flagship Store, China, 2018. Credit: Team Lab Video
119–123, Xiaomi Flagship Store, Shenzhen, China, 2018. Credit: Xiaomi.
124, 125, Litro, Romania, 2009. Photography by Stefan Panfili.
126, Litro, Romania, 2009. Image by Eight Inc.
127, 128, Litro, Romania, 2009. Photography by Stefan Panfili.
142–145, Globe Live, Manila, 2018. Photography by Nascasa & Partners.
146, Globe Gen3 Retail, Manila, 2018. Photography by Nascasa & Partners.
147, Globe Live, Manila, 2018. Photography by Nascasa & Partners.
148–151, Chapel Street Plaza, Melbourne, 2020. Renderings by Vis-Lab.
152–155, Lincoln, China, 2015. Credit: Lincoln China Team.
156–160, Xiao Guan Tea Retail Store, Jinan, China, 2016. Photography by Wei Xuliang.
165, Eight Inc. Experience Realm © 2005 Eight Inc.
178, 179, Apple Genius Bar, Tokyo, 2003. Credit: Apple.
180, 181, Apple Store, London, 2004. Credit: Apple.
182, Apple Store Fifth Avenue, New York, 2006. Credit: Apple.
183, Apple Store, New York, 2007. Credit: Apple.
184, Apple Mini Store, Palo Alto, 2001. Credit: Apple.
185, Apple Mini Store, Palo Alto, 2001. Credit: Apple.
186, 187, Apple Store, Paris, 2012. Credit: Apple.
188, Apple Store, San Francisco, 2013. Credit: Apple.
189, Apple Store, London, 2013. Credit: Apple.
190, 191, OUE Re:Store Branding, Singapore, 2016. Credit: OUE.
192, 193, OUE Re:Store Branding, Singapore, 2016. Image by Eight Inc. Singapore.
194, 195 Two Rooms Grill Bar, Tokyo, 2019. Credit: Two Rooms Grill Bar.
196, 197, Coach Ginza Flagship Store, Tokyo, 2004. Credit: Coach.

198–200, Gap Ginza, Tokyo, 2011. Credit: Gap.
214–219, Nissan Crossing, Tokyo, 2016. Photography by Nascasa & Partners.
220–223, SingEx, Singapore, 2016. Renderings by Vis-Lab.
224 JR Vending Machine, Tokyo, 2010. Source: https://dunia.tempo.co
225 (top image), JR Vending Machine, Tokyo, 2010. Source: https://dunia.tempo.co
225 (bottom image), JR Vending Machine, Tokyo, 2010. Source: Video (00:56), by Bartholo Alexandre.
226–231, Weltmeister Maker Lab, China, 2018. Credit: Eight Inc.
232–235, Jumeirah Website, 2009. Credit: Eight Inc.
236–239, Nokia Flagship Store, Sao Paulo, 2008. Credit: Nokia.
240, Nokia Consumer Electronic Show, Las Vegas, 2008. Credit: Nokia.
250, 251, Citibank, London, 2011. Credit: Citibank.
252–255, Citi Private Bank InView, New York, 2014. Image by Eight Inc.
256–261, Airtel Next-Gen Retail Program, India, 2017. Photography by Nascasa & Partners.
262, 263, S20 Bank, Seoul, 2012. Renderings by Eight Inc.
264–267, Akbank, Istanbul, 2018. Photography by Eight Inc.
268, 269, Citibank, Tokyo, 2009. Credit: Citibank.
270–272, Citibank, New York, 2010. Credit: Citibank.
286–291, Notre Dame Proposal, Paris, 2019. Renderings by Vis-Lab.
292, Polaris Packaging, 2014. Credit: Eight Inc.
293, 294, Polaris Brand Book, 2014. Credit: Eight Inc.
295, Polaris Digital Communications, 2014. Credit: Eight Inc.
296–301, Felissimo Headquarters, Kobe, 2018. Renderings by Vis-Lab.
302–308, Guazi Flagship Store, Chengdu, 2018. Photography by Wei Xuliang 魏徐亮.
320, *The New Algorithm of Value* by Professor Scott Galloway. Source: L2.
322–325, Nam June Paik Museum, Seoul, 2004. Renderings by Eight Inc.
326–331, Keepland, Beijing, 2019. Photography by Keep.
332, 333, Storelli, New York, 2003. Photography by Scott Morris, SGM Photography.
334, 335, Suiki Lor Branding, San Francisco, 2016. Credit: Eight Inc. Singapore.
336–339, Malama Learning Center, Hawaii, 2013. Renderings by Vis-Lab.
342–344, Edgewood Residence, Mill Valley, 2003. Photography by Tim Hursley.
354, 355, Nike Zoom Lebron IV Launch, New York, 2007. Credit: Nike.
356, 357, Swatch Olympic Pavilion, Atlanta, 1996. Credit: Swatch.
358, 359, Swatch Olympic Pavilion, Atlanta, 1996. Photography by Magic Monkey.
360–363, Singtel FutureNow, Singapore, 2019. Photography by Nascasa & Partners.
364–367, Dolby Cinema, Eindhoven, 2014. Credit: Dolby Cinema.
368, 369, Tomorowww, Global, 2015. Images by Eight Inc.
370, 371, Art Intelligence, Global, 2012. Credit: Art Intelligence.
372, 373, Guazi Headquarter Office, Beijing, 2018. Photography by Zhang Boran 张博然, Eric.
374, 375, Donors Choose.org, New York, 2014. Photography by Scott Morris, SGM Photography.
376, INSEAD Creative Garage, Singapore, 2016. Photography by Colin Wee.
390–395, Drop Zone, Dubai, 2014. Renderings by Eight Inc.
396–399, Union Larder, San Francisco, 2014. Photography by Gundolf Pfotenhauer.
400–403, Oslo National Museum of Art, Oslo, 2009. Renderings by Eight Inc.
404–407, Bently Heritage Distillery, Minden, 2019. Photography by Bently Heritage Distillery.
408, Lissa Flatware, Dansk, 1994. Photography by Erik Anderson for Eight Inc.
418, 419, Eight Inc. Studio, San Francisco, 2011. Credit: Eight Inc.

Publications

29, 40, 41, 62, Kevin Kaiser and S. David Yang. "What Managing For Value Really Means," *The Blue Line Emperative,* 2013.

67, Bruce Temkin. "Experience Matters," *Temkin Group Research,* 2018.

94, 97, Chris Pemberton. "Customer Experience Survey," *Gartner,* 2018.

97, 320, Scott Galloway. "The Original Algorithm of Value," *L2,* 2017.

102, Jacques Bughin, Jonathan Doogan, Ole Jørgen Vetvik. "A new way to measure word-of-mouth marketing," *McKinsey & Company,* 2010.

143, James Allen, Frederick F. Reichheld, Barney Hamilton and Rob Markey. "Closing the Delivery Gap," Bain & Company, 2005.

167, 170, Joseph Pine II. "The Experience Economy," *Strategic Horizons*, 1999.

168, Linda A. Hill, Greg Brandeau, Emily Truelove, Kent Lineback. "Collective Genius," *Harvard Business Review,* 2014.

168, Mark J. Perry. "Fortune 500 Firms 1995 v. 2017," *Fortune 500,* 2017.

170, Harris Poll. "Millenials Fueling the Experience Economy," *EventBrite,* 2014.

202, 215, Simon Sinek. "The Golden Circle, "*Start With Why,* 2009.

209, 210, Marcus Fairs. "Dezeen Book of Interviews," *Dezeen,* 2013.

381, Andrew J. Oswald, Eugenio Proto, Daniel Sgroi. "Happiness and Productivity," *Warwick,* 2015.

ORO Editions
Publishers of Architecture, Art, and Design
Gordon Goff: Publisher

www.oroeditions.com
info@oroeditions.com

Published by ORO Editions

By Tim Kobe
with Roger Lehman

Edited by Dylan Parry
Designed by Abdul Basit Khan & Yoana Wiman
Managing Editor: Jake Anderson

10 9 8 7 6 5 4 3 2 1 First Edition

ISBN: 978-1-935935-67-4

Color Separations and Printing: ORO Group Ltd.
Printed in China.

ORO Editions makes a continuous effort to minimize the overall carbon footprint of its publications. As part of this goal, ORO Editions, in association with Global ReLeaf, arranges to plant trees to replace those used in the manufacturing of the paper produced for its books. Global ReLeaf is an international campaign run by American Forests, one of the world's oldest nonprofit conservation organizations. Global ReLeaf is American Forests' education and action program that helps individuals, organizations, agencies, and corporations improve the local and global environment by planting and caring for trees.